LIFE IN ANCIENT INDIA

LIFE IN ANCIENT INDIA

Studies in Rig Vedic India

By

Adolf Kaegi

Translated from the German by

R. Arrowsmith Ph.D.

GYAN

Published by

GYAN

Gyan Publishing House
5, Ansari Road
Daryaganj, New Delhi-110002
Phone: 011-47034999, 9811692060
E-mail: books@gyanbooks.com

Distribution Network
gyanbooks.com
India, USA, Canada, UK, Australia, France

ISBN : 978-81-212-2572-4 (HB)
First Published, 1950

2nd Impression 2021

Printed at: Gyan Press, Delhi.

Life in Ancient India
Author: Adolf Kaegi

LIFE IN ANCIENT INDIA

Studies in Rig Vedic India

by

ADOLF KAEGI

Translated from the German by

R. ARROWSMITH Ph.D.

SUSIL GUPTA (INDIA) LTD.
CALCUTTA

CONTENTS

PAGE

INTRODUCTION

It is well known with what enthusiasm Voltaire, in his writings, especially in the *Essay on the Manners and Spirit of Nations*,[1] repeatedly praised the ancient wisdom of the Brâhmaṇas which he thought to have discovered in the *Yajurvedam*, brought to his notice from India about the middle of the last century. But even Voltaire's eloquence persuaded but few of his contemporaries of the authenticity of the book. Although scholars were not in a position to disprove its genuineness, they preserved a suspicious and sceptical attitude toward it. Soon after Voltaire's death, J. G. Herder, in the tenth book of his *Ideas on the History of Mankind*,[2] unhesitatingly expressed his opinion that whatever knowledge Europeans had hitherto gained of the mysteries of the Indians, was plainly only modern tradition; "for the real Veda of the Indians," he adds, "as well as for the real Sanskrit language, we shall probably have long to wait." Although, happily, Herder's prophecy as to the language itself was not fulfilled, yet in fact a number of decades passed before more trustworthy and detailed information was gained of these oldest literary memorials of the Indians. Colebrooke's celebrated *Essays On the Vedas* did indeed (in 1805) give a valuable survey of the whole territory of the Vedic literature, with some scattered quotations from various Vedic books; but it was not possible for Colebrooke to examine all the extraordinarily extensive works which are embraced in India under the name *Veda*, to distinguish properly the individual writings, or to determine their mutual relations.

About twenty years later a German, Friedrich Rosen, recognised in the rich collection of Vedic manuscripts which had come to London, in great part through the efforts of Colebrooke, the true worth of this literature, and the need of making it accessible to European scholarship. He undertook with zeal the editing of the oldest portion, the Rigveda, but died in 1837, before the first eighth was published.

The first enduring impulse was given by the small but epoch-making *On the Literature and History of the Vedas,*[3] von Rudolph Roth, Stuttgart, 1846. It inaugurated a movement which since then has irresistibly led all Sanskritists to the study of the Veda. As early as 1852, aided by the recent purchase of a rich collection of Sanskrit manuscripts by the Royal Library of Berlin, A. Weber was enabled to give, in his *Studies in Indian Literary History*[4] a very detailed and valuable survey of the Vedic books, which was afterwards supplemented in many points, especially for the later periods, by Max Muller's *History of Ancient Sanskrit Literature,* London, 1859. During the last twenty years, through the efforts of Benfey, Weber, Roth and Whitney, and Aufrecht, the most important texts, since followed by many more, have been accessible in printed form; and this investigation opens to the historical sciences, in the broadest sense of the word, sources of unexpected wealth.

VEDIC LITERATURE

VEDA is primarily 'knowledge' in general, and among the Indians designates knowledge—the sacred knowledge,—the sacred writings, of which a brief survey follows.

The oldest division, the MANTRA (saying, song), is distributed in four *Saṃhitâs* (collections),—the *Rig, Sâma-Yajur-*, and *Atharva-Saṃhitâs.* The oldest and most valuable portion of these collections, the foundation of the whole Vedic literature, is composed of songs, in which, in primeval times, at the first stage of their history as an independent nationality, still at the threshold of the land which they afterward filled with their culture,—more than 1000 years before the expedition of Alexander the Great in the same regions, centuries before the production of the Indian Pantheism or of the gods Brahmâ, Vishnu, Śiva,—in which that people in childlike simplicity praised and entreated their gods, with which they accompanied their sacrifices and strove to propitiate the revered ruler of their destiny, to gain for themselves and their flocks prosperity and secure habitations. From the whole treasury of song which, as its best possession, the Indian race had brought with it from earlier homes to the land of the Ganges, learned men and teachers in later centuries made a selection of the hymns, which had already become partially unintelligible; these they divided, arranged, and used in their schools. Such a selection has been preserved to us, viz.:

The *Rigveda;* the knowledge of the hymns which will be considered more at length below. It was made with the intention of protecting this heritage of ancestral times from further corruption, and from destruction; and is therefore, to an extent, a scientific, historical collection, while the two following *saṃhitâs* had their origin in practical, liturgical uses.

The *Sâmaveda*, the knowledge of the songs, contains about 1800 separate verses, for the greater part taken from the hymns of the *Rig*, but here torn out of their original relation and put together almost without any internal connection. Remodelled with certain musical modifications, they are called *sâman*, songs, in which form they were recited at the Soma sacrifice[5] by a special priest-class, whose song-book therefore this Veda is. By the musical modification of single verses, the whole number of *Sâman* could naturally be greatly increased.

The *Yajurveda* contains the knowledge of the prayers. When in time the sacrifice became no longer a simple act of divine worship and offering, left to the free-will and impulse of the individual, but when more and more in every detail an established ritual was set up, the exact observance of which fell to various priest-classes, not only the verses to be recited during the ceremony, but also a quantity of formulas and phrases of explanation, of excuse, blessing, etc., for practical use, began to be put together. Such words, formulas, and passages, partly in connected, partly in unconnected form, among them, too, not a few verses from the *Rig*, were called *Yajus;* and the books containing the *Yajus* for the whole sacrificial ceremony, *Yajurveda*. We hear of a considerable number of such prayer-books; two of them, related in contents, but differing in arrangement, have already been edited; a third, in all probability the oldest of the existing ones, has been disclosed only within the last few years.[6] The composition of all these books belongs to a period when the priest-class had already gained a decided ascendancy over the other classes.

It was only at a time considerably later than these collections (*trayî vidyâ,* threefold knowledge), that a fourth attained to canonical recognition, the *Atharva-* or *Brahmaveda,* knowledge of incantations. This probably contained originally the poetry more properly belonging to the people and current among them, which only secondarily was admitted into the circle of the priests, and distributed among their productions. As a historical collection of songs it has most similarity to the Rigveda, though the spirit of the two collections is quite different. 'The *Rig* is permeated by a lively sympathy and love of nature; in the *Atharvan* rule only shrinking dread of its evil spirits and their magic powers'. The word *Bráhman* (whence *Brahmaveda*), here means no longer, as in the *Rig,* 'devotion, prayer,' but 'charm, spell, enchantment (song, incantation, devotion)'. By the use of such a formula the skilled priest is enabled to attain everything, and to force even the gods to the fulfillment of his will. Side by side with later passages are found here many formulas, whose perfect agreement with Old-Germanic spells reveals their origin from the ancient Indo-Germanic period. Of this Veda too a new recension has lately become known, and with it a considerable quantity of new Vedic texts.

The second grand division of Vedic literature is formed by the *Brâhmaṇa, i.e.,* writings relating to *Bráhman,* to prayer and sacrificial ceremony.[7] These clearly belong to a much later period, when the old hymns were regarded as ancient and sacred revelation, acquaintance with which was confined to a small number of wise priestly teachers, among whom, however, even at this period, its interpretation was a matter of strife, because the language had meantime become a different one. The *Brâhmaṇas,* all of them marvellous products of priestly knowledge and perverted imagination, are throughout in prose, and for the greater part, like the *Saṃhitâs,* furnished with accents. They develop the theories of celebrated teachers concerning the sense of the old hymns, their relation to the sacrifices, the symbolic meaning of the latter, etc. Dogma, mythology, legend, philosophy, exegesis, etymology, are here interwoven in reckless confusion. Since these works furnish the oldest prescriptions for the ritual and explanation of the language, as well as the oldest traditions and philosophical speculations, they are not without value for the history of language and civilization; but the gold is largely hidden under a mass of dross.

The *Brâhmaṇas* themselves, of which a considerable number are preserved, are in later times looked upon as inspired, and united with the hymns as *śruti,* revelation, excepting only the youngest portions, the Āraṇyakas, writings for the wood-dwellers,[8] and the Upanishads, instructions. Both classes of works show a method of thought totally different from that of the old Vedic books; and with their speculations on cosmogony and eschatology lead into the midst of the system of the *Vedânta* ('aim or end of Veda'). Muller says: "Next follow the Āraṇyakas which, not only by the position which they occupy at the end of the Brâhmanas, but also by their character, seem to be of a later age again. Their object is to show how sacrifices may be performed by people living in the forest, without any of the pomp described in the Brâhmaṇas and the later Sûtras —by a mere mental effort. The worshipper had only to imagine the sacrifice, to go through it only in his memory, and he thus acquired the same merit as the performer of tedious rites. Lastly come the Upanishads; and what is their object? To show the utter uselessness, nay, the mischievousness, of all ritual performances; to condemn every sacrificial act which has for its motive a desire or hope of reward; to deny, if not the existence, at least, the exceptional and exalted character of the Devas, and to teach that there is no hope of salvation and deliverance, except by the individual Self recognizing the true and universal Self, and finding rest there, where alone rest can be found."

The third and youngest stage of Vedic literature is the *Vedânga* ('members of the Veda'), also called SUTRA. The more Vedic study gained in extent, the more difficult it became to master it. 'The mass of material became too large; the fullness of description in details had to yield to a short survey of the sum of these details, in which the greatest brevity was necessary'. Therefore the most concise rules were invented with a conventional system for the designation of termini technici, expressed in algebraic formula. These rules, as well as the books embracing them in almost unbroken succession, are called *Sûtra* (thread, guide, rule); they do not confine themselves to one school or recension, and, especially in later times, attain the last imaginable degree of brevity. How far this principle was pushed may be seen from the saying of the Indian scholars, that "an author should rejoice as much over the saving of half a long vowel as over the birth of a son"; in which it must be remembered that without a son to perform the death rites, a Brâhmaṇa was not thought capable of gaining heaven. We must confine ourselves to mentioning the six *Vedânga-* or *Sûtra*-groups in the traditional order, and to pointing out briefly their signification. They are:

1. *Śikshâ*: pronunciation.
2. *Chandas*: metre.
3. *Vyâkaraṇa*, (lit. 'analysis'): grammar.
4. *Nirukta* (word-explanation): etymology.
5. *Kalpa*: ritual.
6. *Jyotisha*: astronomy.

The first four are chiefly occupied with the reading

and understanding of the sacred texts; the last two principally with the sacrifice and its seasons.

As from the study of Homer the Greek grammar rose, so from the study of the Veda grew the Indian; but the investigations of the Indians, favoured by the constitution of their language, were incomparably deeper and more lasting than those of the Greek grammarians. Prominent among the grammatical writings are the *Nirukta*, a collection of strange or obscure words of the Veda, together with the interpretation of the Vedic investigator *Yâska* (about 500 B.C.), and the *Prâtiśâkhyas*, each of which contains, for the various recensions of a single Veda, the most precise statements of phonetic changes, pronunciation, accentuation, metre, etc. In connection, they display a number of delicate observations in phonetics, such as only the science of our own day has begun to institute and turn to account.[9] The above named works therefore do not treat of grammatical forms; of older works on this subject little has been left us, clearly because a later work, in its comprehensive and practical presentation surpassed all earlier ones and made them superfluous; namely, the grammar of *Pâṇini*, who probably lived in the third century B.C. "In them is presented the scientific treatment of a single tongue in a perfection which arouses the wonder and admiration of all those who are more thoroughly acquainted with it; which even now stands, not only unsurpassed, but not even attained, and which in many respects may be looked upon as the model for similar work. In this presentation of the Sanskrit the method of the Indian grammarians was displayed; and it found so much the more speedy acceptance, since it is nearly allied to the tendency which since the beginning of this century has made itself felt with ever increasing power in other sciences. This is the method applied to the natural sciences; the method which seeks to gain knowledge of a subject from itself, by analysis into its elements. It views language as a natural phenomenon, the character of which it strives to determine by analysis into its component parts and investigation of their functions; by this method and its wonderful results the linguistic labours of the Indians have pre-eminently,—indeed, almost alone,—made it possible for modern philology to take up its problem and work it out to its end with the success which is universally conceded to it".—(*Benfey*).

The treatises on Ritual, the Kalpasûtras, specially called Sûtra, are either:

1. *Srautasûtra* (pertaining to *śruti*, revelation); *i.e.*, they contain the prescriptions for the solemn ceremonies to be performed with the assistance of the priests and with exact observance of the ritual; or

2. *Smârtasûtra* (pertaining to *smṛiti*, tradition); *i.e.*, they teach the observances prescribed by tradition, and are divided into (*a*) *Gṛhyasûtra*, giving the models for acts of domestic piety which must accompany the individual and his family in all special circumstances of life from the cradle to the grave; these books, though made later, preserve many ancient characteristics;[10] and into (*b*) *Dhârmasûtra*, which fix the rules of daily life in act and attitude toward others; from these last arose later the metrical law-books (*Dharmaśâstra*) of Manu, Yâjnavalkya, and others.

There are, finally, a number of additions (*Parisishṭa*), among which I mention the Purâṇas ('old tales'), which in their present form date at the earliest from the eighth century A.D., only because, up to the fourth decade of the present century,—(with some "historians" even later!)—they ranked with the Upanishads as the most important source of 'Indian' and 'Vedic' religious conceptions.

Upon the whole of this rich literature, which in extent at least equals all the preserved monuments of the Greek literature, essentially rest the commentaries of *Mâdhava* and *Sâyaṇa*, still preserved and highly regarded in India, which however were only composed in the fourteenth century A.D. About 1350, in the middle of the Deccan, in the Karṇâṭa territory, a man of humble, non-Aryan descent succeeded in throwing off the Mohammedan yoke and in setting up in those regions once more and for the last time a magnificent Indian nation, by founding the dynasty of Vijayanagara (city of Victory). At the court of the third king of this dynasty, Bukka, the prime minister, Mâdhava, and his brother Sâyaṇa instituted an intense and widespread scientific activity, to which we owe, among many other works, these Vedic commentaries or paraphrases.

What then is more natural than, at the time when the Veda was beginning to be understood, when a wholly new world was here unfolding to view, the understanding of which however presented at the outset the very greatest difficulties,—what more natural than that aid should eagerly be sought, which might serve for the interpretation of this unknown material! It was a matter of rejoicing that works were at once found explaining or paraphrasing every word of the foundation text; and as they appeal at every step to old authorities, it was believed that in them lay not *a* tradition or traditional explanation, but *the* tradition,—the true interpretation from ancient times. The problem of Vedic investigation was considered to be the search for and discovery of that interpretation which was current in India a few centuries ago, *i.e.*, the interpretation presented in the commentaries.

A. Weber remarks: "Such passages, and others of similar character,—and there is a number of them,—should be noticed by those who still consider that Vedic interpretation according to the Indian method is preferable to our own, freeing itself in essentials from the native method. Whoever has carefully studied the Indian interpretations knows that absolutely no continuity of tradition can be assumed between the production of the Vedas and their interpretation by Indian scholars; that on the contrary between the genuine poetical remains of Vedic antiquity and their interpretation a long break must have occurred in the tradition, out of which, at the most, the understanding of a few details may have been preserved up to later times, through liturgical uses and words, passages, and perhaps also hymns connected with it. Beyond these remains of the tradition, which must be estimated at a very small value, the interpreters of the Veda had almost no other aids than those which are in great part at our own disposal, the usage of the classical language and the grammatical, etymological, lexical investigations. At most they found assistance in matter preserved in dialects; but this advantage is almost entirely outweighed by that which we have at command, the comparison with Zend and with the other languages related to the Sanskrit, which, while it must of course be applied with care and discrimination, has already afforded so much help to clearer understanding of the Vedas. But independently of all aids in particular cases, through the confusion with which it seeks to comprehend from its own religious standpoint, so many centuries later, the ancient conditions and conceptions completely foreign to it, the Indian interpretation comes to be false throughout its whole spirit; while we, through our knowledge, drawn from analogous conditions, of the life, conceptions, and needs of ancient peoples and of popular poetry, are better equipped for an understanding of the whole; and this superiority, even if the Indians owed much more in details to tradition than they really do, would not be dimmed by their interpretation."

On the other hand, Roth insisted from the beginning that these commentaries could by no means be taken as the chief guides, for we have to seek not the sense which these books attribute to the hymns, but that which the composers themselves intended; that these works might indeed be excellent guides to the understanding of the theological books and the ritual, but altogether insufficient in the far older and entirely different territory of the hymns; that concerning the latter there was nowhere a trace of views handed down by tradition, *i.e.*, of continuity in the interpretation, but only a tradition among investigators. But that any other tradition was not imaginable; for it only began to be asked how one point or another in the old hymns was to be interpreted, when they were no longer, or at least no longer clearly, understood;[11] that we have in the so-called tradition only attempts at a solution, not the solution itself; that in discovering the latter, European scholars would succeed much better than Indian theologians, having the advantage in freedom of judgement, as well as in a larger range of view and historical faculty. However, Roth expressed himself thus only on occasion, but boldly and independently began to build anew. By the aid of grammatical and etymological comparison, by confronting all passages related in sense and form, he endeavoured, keeping in view the tradition, to evolve the meaning of single words, and so created a broad and firm foundation for Vedic exegesis; while others, partly in more negative manner proved the impracticability of the native interpretation, partly went forward on the road newly pointed out. The correctness of the method is to-day no longer challenged by any non-Indian scholar; even in India itself within a few years the publication of an edition of the Rig-veda has been undertaken which more and more makes independent use of the results and methods of European scholarship. But no one disputes that we have not yet by far reached the foundation; and none better know this than those who are zealously striving, on the path pointed out and with continual observance of the native tradition, to further, by minute investigation of particulars, the understanding of these ancient hymns. All these corrections will in no measure detract from the services of the founder of Vedic exegesis. 'That Roth has cut his way through the fog of Indian misinterpretation straight to the kernel of the Veda, that he has seized with sure historical sense the spirit of Indian antiquity, that he has taught us to recognize the power and freshness of expression, of which the Indians knew little more,—this is one of the most brilliant archievements of modern philology'. (*Delbrück*).

THE VEDIC PEOPLE AND ITS CIVILIZATION

AFTER this general literary and historical introduction, we must preface our special subject, the examination of the Rigveda, with some account of the people among whom the book arose, of its life and occupation, its manner of action and thought. In this we may throughout rely on Zimmer's excellent work,[12] which presents a masterly picture of the culture of the Vedic Aryans, drawn from all the Saṃhitâs.

To comparative philology we owe the indisputable proof of the fact that the ancestors of Indians and Iranians and Greeks, of Slavs and Lithuanians and Germans, of Italians and Celts, in far distant ages spoke one language, and as a single people held dwelling-places in common, wherever that home may have been situated;[13] and further, that for a considerable period after their separation from their brothers living further to the west, the Indians and Iranians lived together, and distinguished themselves from other tribes by the common name of Aryan. After their separation from the Iranians, the Eastern Aryans, the later Indians, wandered from the west into the land afterwards called *India*, descending from the heights of Iran, probably over the western passes of the Hindukush. As to their place of abode at the time of composition of most of the hymns of the Rig—about 2000-1500 B.C.[14]—the names of rivers mentioned in the hymns give definite information. According to these, the chief settlement of the Vedic people was then in the territory of the Sindhu (to-day *Indus, Sindh*), the banks of the mighty stream itself being probably most thickly populated, the river, after receiving all its tributaries, reaching so great a width that boats midway between its shores are invisible from either. The singers in inspired strains sing its greatness: "With nourishing waves it rushed forth, a firm stronghold and brazen fortress for us; like a fighter in his chariot, the stream flows on, overtaking all others. It alone among the rivers flows with pure water from the mountains to the sea; with regard for riches, for many men, it brings fatness and a refreshing draught to the dwellers on the shore".

Simple tribes, like the Gandhâri still remained in the valley of the Kubhâ (*Kabul*) and the Suvâstu (*Swat*), a northern tributary; to the south the settlements had been pushed beyond the mouths of the Krumu (*Kurum*) and Gomatî (*Gomal*), but not far beyond the union of the Sindhu with the *Pancanada*,[15] though they knew of the Sindhu's emptying into the ocean. In the north, the western and middle Himâlaya formed an impassable wall; to the east the Śutudrî (*Satlej*) must for a long time have formed the boundary, across which from time to time they moved forward to the Yamunâ (*Jumna*) and Gangâ (*Ganges*), enticed by the beauty of the land and pressed on by advancing tribes behind.

In East Kabulistan and the Punjab, therefore, where the condition of climate and soil was about the same as now, the Aryan colonists lived in their houses; for they had already changed the movable tent of the shepherd and nomad for a more fixed shelter. "Columns were set up on firm ground, with supporting beams leaning obliquely against them, and connected by rafters on which long bamboo rods were laid, forming the high roof. Between the corner-posts other beams were set up, according to the size of the house. The crevices in the walls were filled in with straw or reeds, tied in bundles, and the whole was to some extent covered with the same material. The various parts were fastened together with bars, pegs, ropes and thongs". The house could be shut in by a door, which, as in the Homeric houses, was fastened with a strap. A number of such dwellings form the village; fenced and enclosed settlements give protection against wild animals; against the attacks of enemies and against inundations large tracts were arranged on higher ground, protected by earthworks and ditches. But of cities, *i.e.*, of collections of adjoining houses, surrounded by wall and moat, there is no mention.

The principal means of sustenance was cattle-keeping. Repeatedly in the hymns we meet with the prayer for whole herds of cows and horses, sheep and goats, heifers and buffaloes, but especially of milch-cows, which are to more than one singer the sum of 'all good which Indra has created for our enjoyment'. By divine power the red cow yields the white milk, from which is prepared mead and butter, 'the favourite food of gods and men', and perhaps also cheese. After the cattle, the most important interest is the cultivation of the soil. The ground is worked with plough and harrow, mattock and hoe, and when necessary watered by means of artificial canals. Twice in the year the products of the field, especially barley, ripen; the grain is threshed on the floor, the corn, separated from husk and chaff by the winnowing, is ground in the mill and made into bread. Men still engage in hunting game with bow and arrow, snares and traps, but this occupation has no importance as a means of livelihood, and fishing still less. The chief food consists, together with bread, of various preparations of milk, cakes of flour and butter, many sorts of vegetables and fruits; meat, cooked on the spit or in pots, is little used, and was probably eaten only at the great feasts and family gatherings. Drinking plays throughout a much more prominent part than eating. "The waters are indeed pre-eminently praised; in them lie all healing properties, and they secure to the body, health, protection and long-continued sight of the sun;—but it no more occurred to the Vedic people to quench their thirst with water than to the ancient Germans. They bathed in it, and the cattle drank it; man had other beverages,"—*surâ,* a brandy made from corn or barley, and above all, the sorrow-dispelling Soma, which, on account of its inspiring power, was raised to the position of a god, and will therefore be considered below.

Among occupations that of the wood-worker is most frequently mentioned; he is still carpenter, wheelwright and joiner in one, and is skilled not only in building war-chariots and wagons with all their parts, but also in more delicate carved work, such as artistic cups, etc. The tanner prepares leather from the hide of the slaughtered cattle, and uses it for water-bottles, bow-strings, slings and other articles. Metal-workers, smiths and potters ply their craft for the purposes of common life. Navigation, being confined to the streams of the Punjab, could not be very important, and trade exists only as barter, the foundation of which, as well as the money unit, is the cow, in reference to which all things are valued. But the transition to the use of coined money was being prepared by the various golden ornaments and jewellery; active tradesmen and usurers come to view; while the occurrence of the Babylonian mina as an accepted gold standard proves, in connection with other facts, a very early intercourse between Indian and the western Semitic colonies.

The women understood the plaiting of mats, weaving and sewing; they manufactured the wool of the sheep into clothing for men and covering for animals, and were especially occupied with their many ornaments and decorations.

The foundation of the state was formed by the Family, at the head of which stood the father as lord of the house. The foundation of a family proceeded from the man. At festal gatherings and similar occasions there were often opportunities for forming acquaintance between youth and maiden, and even then careful mothers did not neglect, at such times, to come to their daughters' assistance with advice and action. If such an acquaintance proved lasting, permission for the marriage had to be sought from the father or, after his death, from the eldest brother. This office was assumed by a friend of the suitor, who is always the oldest unmarried son of a family, for it was a settled custom for the children of a family to marry in order of age. If the suitor was acceptable, he had to purchase his bride by rich gifts to his future father-in-law. Thereupon the marriage was celebrated in traditional form in the presence of both families and their friends in the house of the bride's parents. Further on we shall have opportunity for a fuller description of the ceremony. That a marriage portion was given with the young wife is not distinctly stated but is yet indicated, as also that a rich inheritance helped many a girl to gain a husband, who otherwise would have remained in her father's house. In the new home the young wife is subject to her husband, but at the same time mistress of the farm-labourers and slaves, and of parents—and brothers-in-law. The Vedic singers know no more tender relation than that between the husband and his willing, loving wife, who is praised as "his home, the darling abode and bliss in his house". The high position of the wife is above all shown by the fact that she participates in the sacrifice with her husband; with harmonious mind at the early dawn both, in fitting words, send up their prayers to the Eternals. These relations are comprehensible only if monogamy was the rule; and to this the texts point directly. Though there were instances of polygamy, especially among kings and nobles, yet the ordinary condition was "a united pair, with one heart and one mind, free from discord". Marriage was looked upon as an arrangement founded by the gods, the aim of which was the mutual support of man and wife and the propagation of their race; therefore it is the often-repeated wish of the Vedic singer to beget a son of his own flesh, whose place could never be filled by adoption; while the birth of a daughter is nowhere distinctly desired, but is even plainly asked to be averted. That exposure of new-born children and of old people enfeebled by age occurs offends our feelings no more than the well-known custom of burning the widows, for thousands of years demanded by the Brâhmaṇas. The latter, it is true, is nowhere evidenced in the Rigveda; only by palpable falsification of a hymn, which will be examined later, has the existence of the custom been forcibly put into the texts, which, on the contrary, prove directly the opposite,—the return of the widow from her husband's corpse into a happy life, and her re-marriage. Yet from other indications we have to accept the probability that the custom, which in the oldest times was widespread, of causing the widow to follow her husband to death, was also observed now and then in the Vedic period. Such features might easily modify our general verdict regarding the stage of morality and culture of the Vedic Aryans; but we must not forget that "people in a condition of nature are not sentimental, as to-day peasants are not; and that the death of a relative, or the thought of their own, leaves them indifferent". When, in addition to what has been said above of the tender relation between husband and wife, we learn that violence to defenceless maidens and unfaithfulness on the part of a married woman belong to the heaviest offences, we must infer that true womanliness and morality generally prevailed. It is a matter of course that the picture had its shadows. Even at that time the woman was charged with fickleness, light-mindedness, and lack of judgment; mention is here and there made of the sons of unmarried women; fallen ones tried to free themselves from the consequences of their misdeeds in criminal manner, and even prostitutes were not wanting.

On the foundation of the family rests the State, the organization of which in the Vedic period is very near that of the primitive times. For protection against threatened attacks and for the purpose of marauding incursions into the territory of other peoples, coalitions were formed between tribes; but having returned home after a victory, in times of peace the individual people or tribe formed the highest political unit, which was divided into districts, which in turn were composed of single clans or hamlets. The latter were originally, as the expressions in the texts make evident, each a single kindred, a number of families more nearly connected among themselves. This tribe division was applied not only in time of peace but also, as among the Afghans to-day, in battle; warriors of the same families, localities, districts, and tribes fought side by side, in the manner which Tacitus describes as characteristic of the Germans, and as Nestor advises Agamemnon to make his arrangement.

The government of the Aryan states thus organized was naturally, in consequence of their origin in the family, a monarchical, at the head of which the king stands as leader, his dignity being in many instances hereditary. In other cases, he was elected by all the districts in assemblies of the tribe, or in times of peace several members of the royal family exercised the power in common. At all events the kingship was nowhere absolute, but everywhere limited by the will of the people, which made its power felt in assemblies of the nation, the district, and the tribe. In peace the king was "judge and protector" of his people, who owed him lasting obedience but no settled tribute; only voluntary gifts were brought to him. In war he held the chief command and it was his duty, at serious junctures, *e.g.*, before a battle, to prepare a sacrifice for the tribe, either performing it himself or causing a priestly singer to perform it. In this custom of the kings to be represented by a priestly substitute, is to be recognized the beginning of the historically unique Indian hierarchy and the origin of the castes, the existence of which in the oldest Vedic times, in spite of all assertions to the contrary, must be denied.

That developed ideas of Law were present in the oldest period is taught by the common legal terms existing in the various languages of our family. The Vedic texts present a further list of such terms, and the hymns strongly prove how deeply the prominent minds in the people were persuaded that the eternal ordinances of the rulers of the world were as inviolable in mental and moral matters as in the realm of nature, and that every wrong act, even the unconscious, was punished and the sin expiated. But the same hymns also show that the relations of the various members of the community among themselves were not always the best. Deceitful men strove to injure in every way, by slander, lying, and fraud; thieves plied their vocation under the concealing shadow of night; daring swindlers, highwaymen, and robbers terrorized the peaceable and embittered the life of the upright. In cases of doubt as to guilt or the guilty one, recourse was had to oath, on more serious occasions to the decision of the gods in various forms; unworthy men were expelled from the clan and became fugitives. But there are also more pleasing features. Praise is given to those who from their abundance willingly dispense to the needy, to those who do not turn away from the hungry, but who by deeds of kindness to the poor increase their own possessions, and who in change of fortune never swerve from their faithfulness to old friends.

When business is despatched in the assembly, the shrewd men gather together; "they sift their words like corn in a sieve and remember their friendship". Others engage in sport and joking over their drinking, and pour forth irony and boasts or indulge in play with dice, which was passionately loved, and at which many a man gambled away his possessions, and finally even his own person. "Of no effect is the father's punishment of the dissolute son; the player is unmoved by the destruction of his home; he remains indifferent though his wife become the property of others; he rises early and indulges in the passion of play till evening; defeat in play is equivalent to starvation and thirst". Wives and maidens attire themselves in gay robes and set forth to the joyful feast; youths and girls hasten to the meadow when forest and field are clothed in fresh verdure, to take part in the dance. Cymbals sound, and seizing each other lads and damsels whirl about until the ground vibrates and clouds of dust envelop the gaily moving throng.

A more earnest trait appears in the favourite contests in the chariot race, for it is the peaceful preparation for the decisive struggle on the battle-field, for the joyous war in which they delighted, and which plays so large a part in the songs as well as the life of the people. In the battle Indra seeks his friend, battle and struggle give the hero experience and renown, when with his fellow-warriors he helps to conquer new homes or to protect those already won, whether against other Aryans or the hosts of aborigines (*dasyu*), from whom the colonists were sharply separated by different colour, different customs, and above all, by different religion. When an enemy approaches the Aryan boundaries, earthworks are thrown up, a barricade of timbers erected, impassable bulwarks of bronze made, and sacrifices offered to the gods to secure their help. Then the army advances with loud battle-songs, with the sound of drums and trumpets, with waving banners, against the opposing force. The warrior stands at the left of the chariot, and beside him the charioteer, and the foot-soldiers fight in close lines, village beside village, tribe beside tribe. The warrior is protected by brazen coat of mail and helmet; with the bow he hurls against the enemy feathered arrows with poisoned tips of horn or metal, or presses on with spear and axe, lance and sling. And when the enemy is conquered, loud rejoicing resounds with the beat of drums, like the noise of the rising storm; the sacred fire is kindled to offer to the gods a song and sacrifice of thanksgiving, and then to divide the spoil.

In arts and sciences the race still stood on the lowest

stage. The art of writing it did not possess (and even for a long time afterward),[16] and little was known of the ideas of number or of measure. The theories of cosmogony are altogether childish. Among the countless stars certain ones had already been observed and named, before all, the Bear, followed by Sirius and the five planets. The lunar year of 354 days was in various ways brought into harmony with the solar year; either the twelve extra days were added yearly (cf. below) or they were allowed to accumulate, and a thirteenth month from time to time was added to the twelve.—Their medical art distinguished quite a number of diseases, but almost the sole curatives and preventives known were charms and the use of amulets and healing herbs, whose power was brought forth and made effectual only by the sacred formula. Deeper natures indeed only hoped to be freed from their ills by repentance and reformation; for sickness was to them "divinely sent chains" with which Varuna, the world's ruler, bound those who transgressed his eternal laws.

Only one art had long been in full bloom, that of poetry; of this we have the most convincing evidence in that collection of songs, to the more detailed examination of which we now proceed.

THE RIGVEDA

THE COLLECTION—FORM AND CONTENTS OF THE HYMNS

THE recension which has come down to us, the received text of the Śâkala school (*Śâkalaśâkhâ*) contains, in ten books (*Maṇḍala*) 1017 (or 1028) hymns, the extent of which about equals that of the Homeric poems. As a rule, the oldest hymns are contained in Books 2-7; these show only portions, each assigned by tradition to a single family,[17] in which they were long preserved as a family inheritance. These are in order the hymns of Gṛtsamada, Viśvâmitra, Vâmadeva, Atri, Bharadvâja, Vasiṣhṭha and their descendants. The internal arrangement of these Maṇḍalas bear distinct traces of the work of a single school; the hymns in each are arranged in groups according to the gods addressed; and these groups always follow the same order,—first the hymns to Agni, then those to Indra, etc. Inside the groups the position of the hymns is determined by the number of verses in diminishing order; where this principle seems violated, the hymns are either to be separated into shorter ones or they found a place in the collection only at a later date. The eighth book contains chiefly hymns of the Kaṇva gens, but shows no prevailing principle in their arrangement. Book 9 seems to betray a different origin, all its hymns being addressed to one divinity, the inspiring Soma, honoured as a god, and being arranged with reference to the metres. The youngest portion is Books 1 and 10, which, with beautiful examples of Vedic lyrical poetry, also show productions of the latest period of Vedic time, and even of the time of compilation. The fourteen groups of the first book, each hymns of one family, show the same principle in their arrangement as the family books; the tenth shows smaller collections (*e.g.*, liturgical); the whole Maṇḍala gives the impression of a subsequent compilation of religious and secular pieces not collected before.

Since the time at which our collection was closed, about the year 1500 B.C., the text has been handed down, though for centuries orally, with the most painstaking care, so that since that time, nearly 3000 years ago, it has suffered no changes whatever;—with a care such that the history of other literatures has nothing similar to compare with it. The Indians were not satisfied with one form of the text, but made several;[18] grammatical treatises were written upon the mutual relations of the various forms and other like precautions taken. But it is true that at the period of compilation much had become unintelligible; a method of exposition had gained currency which to a certain extent replaced the text, and it is probable that only few hymns then preserved exactly the same form in which they were composed. For example, it is easy to show that in many hymns the order of the verses is changed and that in other verses not belonging to the hymn have been interpolated. Many such erratic portions were collected by the scholiasts in places where from the occurrence of the same or similar words they inferred a similar sense; others show themselves to be modern, and in part very senseless, variations of old hymns or additions made by the priests for the support of their doctrine.

Little need be said of the *external form of the hymns;* this language is an exceedingly ancient popular dialect, which differs, in all grammatical points (accentuation, phonetics, word-formation, declension, conjugation, syntax) and in its vocabulary, from the later artificial Indian language, the Sanskrit[19] of the law books, epics, dramas, etc., in a much greater degree than, *e.g.*, the language of Homer from the Attic. Here the wonderful imagery of the language shines out in transparent clearness and exuberance of sparkling brilliancy; its forms of expression are poured forth as from an inexhaustible spring; we meet everywhere originality, richness of diction, pushing growth and buoyant life, which, not yet fettered as in later Sanskrit by the iron-bound canons of a learned grammar, give us glimpses of the development and history of the language, in the laboratory of that immense intellectual product, through which the languages of our family have become the most cultivated of all tongues. In a certain sense this dialect too is artistic; it is, like the language of Homer, though to a smaller degree, a popular artistic or poetic speech developed in the guilds of singers, and the many conventional turns of expression in it plainly prove that the art of song had long been fostered and practised among the people. Here, as in Homer, we often find fixed epithets, formulaic expressions confined to certain connections, rhetorical adornments, idioms and whole passages which repeatedly re-occur unchanged or with slight variations. Assonance, Homoioteleuta, Parachesis and other rhetorical figures, and especially the most varied play upon words, are of frequent application; the refrain, repeating some principal thought, is used with great freedom.

The syntactical relations are usually clear; in the use of case and mode much more of the original fullness of the language is preserved than in Sanskrit or the classical tongues. But since pure Syntax, the developed structure of periods, was not yet matured, it is sometimes impossible to fix upon one or another translation and explanation of a verse as the sole possible and only correct one, even in passages where every individual word is fully clear.

The metrical laws are simple; the stanzas consist throughout of three or more, generally of three or four verses; the latter contain eight, eleven, or twelve syllables, seldom five, more seldom four or more than twelve, and are therefore usually dimeter, trimeter, or trimeter catalectic; the cæsura occurs after the fourth or fifth syllable. The first syllables of the verse are not fixed in regard to quantity (*ancipites*), while the last four are in general strictly measured, iambic in verses of twelve syllables, trochaic in those of eleven; only a few older hymns with verses of eight syllables show a trochaic cadence.[20]

In many hymns two or three stanzas are more closely connected, and thus form a strophe; in others a kind of chain-structure is noticeable, in which the beginning of a stanza or strophe takes up the closing thought of the last stanza or strophe. There are, even at this early date, isolated instances of lyrical dialogue; of which there are also forms which picture the progress of the action and describe past events, and which therefore correspond in nature to the ballad.

As to the CONTENTS, it has already been pointed out above, that the far greater proportion of hymns belongs to the religious lyric; a small number only of secular songs is preserved in the tenth book. The great majority of the hymns are invocations and adoration of the gods respectively addressed; their keynote is a simple outpouring of the heart, a prayer to the eternals, an invitation to them to accept favourably the gift reverently consecrated. Of the later theory of inspiration the hymns recognize nothing. The singer's wish is to give eloquent expression to the sentiments which a god has placed in his soul,—to give vent to the crowding emotions of his heart. "As a skilled workman builds the wagon, like well-adorned and fitted garments he forms his song as best he can according to his knowledge and ability."

Therefore the hymns vary greatly in value; by the side of the splendid productions of divinely inspired poets we find a large number of unimportant, tiresome, and overburdened compositions. But this does not appear strange, when we remember that the Rigveda furnishes us the works of the most various poets of a whole people, some of whom are separated by a period of at least 1000 years; that individual genius is confined neither to locality nor age, and that these productions at the time of compilation, even then partially unintelligible, were looked upon as ancient, divinely inspired wisdom, and therefore protected against all human criticism. Even the flower of the Vedic lyric suffers from monotony and endless repetition, since almost all the hymns are variations of the same theme; but through them all we feel the fresh breath of a vigorous poetry of Nature. If one will only take the trouble to project himself into the life and thought, the poetry and action of a people and age, which best display the first development of intellectual activity in our own race,[31] he will find himself attracted by these hymns on many sides, now by their childlike simplicity, now by the freshness or delicacy of their imagery, and again by the boldness of their painting and their scope of fancy. And most certainly these truly unique literary remains, which throw the strongest light on the most varied conditions of life, of classical as well as present peoples, will remain sealed for all who do not take that trouble,—who are used to recognize a common humanity and pure beauty only when clothed in the most modern forms. They will be closed for all who have never experienced the delight of following back to its distant mountain-sources the mighty river of human thought, on whose surface we ourselves are hastening toward the future, who no longer have any soul for that which has freed the minds of millions of human beings with their noblest hopes, fears, and endeavours; who lack the sense for the History of Humanity.

Turning now to the RELIGIOUS POETRY, we shall not, from what has preceded, expect to find any unified views or defined prevailing conceptions. Each one of the poets so far separated in time follows his own imagination, his individual feeling, his momentary perception, which may conform with those of most of his contemporaries, or may be centuries ahead of them. The whole significance of the *Rigveda* in reference to the general history of religion, as has repeatedly been pointed out in modern times, rests upon this, that it presents to us the development or religious conceptions from the earliest beginnings to the deepest apprehension of the godhead and its relations to man. "Very differently," says L. Geiger, "from all others of the oldest literatures known to us, which show new forms rising on the ruins of a past sunk in oblivion or produced by the contact and commingling of the spiritual characteristics of various peoples, we have in these hymns the picture of an original, primitive life of mankind, free from foreign influences, not restored in new forms from the destruction of the past, but springing forth new and young from the bosom of Nature,—a spiritual form still unspoiled in word and deed; and that which everywhere else we see only as complete and finished, is here presented in process of formation. Therefore in these hymns lies the key to understanding not only the subsequent development of the Indians, nor alone that of all peoples in part springing from the same root, but also, from the unity of nature recognized in the whole process of development of our race, the key to the productions of all speculative power on earth, or to the whole contents of mind, *i.e.*, its lasting acquisitions, from the period when convictions formed from impressions retained in memory first took shape among men, and manifold opinions, beliefs, or knowledge were at all possible".[22]

The Religious Thought is here in greater part filled with the productions of sense. A maze of marvellous stories and myths reveals the mighty influence of the ever-changing phenomena of nature upon the son of earth. The forces of nature impress him now as friends, again as enemies, and he views the wonders of the great creation with the unaccustomed eyes of the child. As a German nursery rhyme asks: "Tell me how white milk can come from the red cow,"—so an Indian sage is struck with wonder that the rough red cow gives soft white milk, and this miracle is praised again and again as an evidence of divine power. There is of course no recognition of the laws of nature, and science does not, as now, spring up at every step as an obstacle to imagination. Now we calculate at what moment a certain star will be visible at a certain spot on the earth, and the rising of the sun causes us no astonishment,—we know that it happens necessarily. Not so the man of that time; when he sees the sun moving freely through the heavens, so evidently producing all life upon the earth, seen and known by all, and yet to all a mystery from beginning to end, what it is, whence it comes, whither it goes,—then he asks:

"Unpropped beneath, not fastened firm, how comes it
That downward turned, he falls not downward?
The guide of his ascending path,—who saw it?"

—4. 13. 5.

Full of wonder he begins to conjecture "whither the Pleiades, that show themselves in the night, go by day," and it seems a miracle to him that "the sparkling waters of all rivers flow into one ocean, without ever filling it."

Such expressions of wonder, if we try to place ourselves in sympathy with the childlike mental conditions of that primitive time, we shall not find childish; we shall rather wonder at the happy and graphic expressions with which man is able to clothe his thoughts when beginning for the first time to grope about him, to perceive, to observe, and from repeated observations to draw conclusions. In all the phenomena of nature he observes movement and action similar to his own or those of his immediate surroundings; but because he never sees movement or action here behind which a moving or acting person does not stand, he logically refers these occurrences in nature to acting persons, who for him coincide with the phenomena. The bright all-containing heaven is him the "Lightener" (*Dyaus*) or the "Surrounder" (*Varuṇa*); the moon is the "Measurer"; the sun, the "Illuminator" (*Sûrya*) or the "Enlivener" (*Savitar*) or the "Nourisher" (*Pûshan*), etc. This silent "wanderer" through space,—this majestic ruler of the firmament,—this friend, departing in the dark West and returning in the shining East, in its daily and yearly courses first showed men an unbroken rule, a strict, unchanging order (*ṛta*). And as the "thinking one" (*mânusha,* man) looks further about him, he observes that, while his own plans are so often crossed and destroyed, while nothing in his daily life has permanency, throughout the whole realm of Nature order, unchangeable and "inimitable," prevails. "In ever-varying alternation with the day-star, the moon light-giving moves through the night; solitary it wanders through the gathering of many; it waxes and wanes; the breathing being of yesterday dies to-day and returns living to-morrow". "Every day, in unceasing interchange with night and her dark wonders, comes the dawn with her bright ones, to reanimate the worlds, never failing in her place, never in her time,—both ever entering on their paths with renewed youth". "Day and night know their seasons, when the dark sister must give place to the bright; they halt not, nor stand still; unlike in colour but of like mind both pursue their endless way," and unchangingly the hot and cold seasons follow each other.

All these occurrences and the forces behind them, these natural phenomena conceived of as personal, are pictured by man as being similar to himself; human in their thinking, feeling, and acting; but, since their order is never disturbed, their will never bent, and their power never broken, infinitely more powerful and exalted and wise; to him they are creatures against whose will no one on earth can contend. As light is to him the symbol of all happiness and blessings, he calls these wise powers, these infallible guardians of the eternal order of the worlds the Shining Ones (*devâs, dívi*), and he adores them as givers of good, as *gods*. In pressing need there rises in his heart a yearning for a helper; he looks about among his kinsmen and companions for aid, but in vain. "Who will take pity, who will give us refreshment, who will come nigh with help? The counsels counsel, the thoughts in the hearts, the wishes wish, they fly out into the worlds; no other merciful one is found but them: therefore my longing lifts itself to the gods". Anxiously the hopeful ask:

"Who is it knows, and who can tell us surely
Where lies the path that leads to the Eternals?
Their deepest dwellings only we discover,
And hidden these in distant secret regions".

—3. 54. 5.

That path the experienced singer has seen, "who sees further than others; he, who has learned to mark the Eternals and in the course of nature to perceive their might and wisdom". He says to mortals that not without effort can gods be gained for friends; the idle and negligent are not pleasing to them; they desire Soma-pressers, constant in prayer and zealous in sacrifice; when the tribes meet in conflict over their possessions, they come as allies to those who offer sacrifices; the Mighty Ones have no friendship for such as bring no gifts. And so man gladly offers the sacrificial food and freely pours the Soma for their enjoyment, and the "span" of his pious songs, that perchance the god may heed and accomplish the singer's wish. With the most pleasing hymns he lays hold on the hem of the Exalted's garments, as a son touches the father's; with loud rejoicing, as the streams rush from the heights, he sends up his devotion to heaven, that the god implored may take it up as the mother clasps the darling son; that he may bind the long rows of songs about him for adornment like the stars in heaven, and rejoice in them as a bridegroom in his bride. Superficial natures, indeed, naively think to talk the gods over: "If I possessed as much as you, O God, I would not give the singer over to poverty, and day by day would give my adorer rich possessions, wherever he might be." "If you were a mortal and I immortal, I would not abandon you to misfortune nor poverty; my singer would not be needy, not in evil case, not lacking his deserts."

Another, oppressed by heavy trouble, turns to the lord of the old home, to whom his father called,—to that god who has so often aided before, the support of the sacrificer and the friend of his ancestors, who rejoices in being implored, and who cares for him like a loving father; for he knows from experience: "If I asked again and again, the ever victorious Indra fulfilled all my prayers".

And if unable to offer an ox or cow, he hopes that

even small gifts from the heart, a fagot, a libation, a bundle of grass, offered with reverence, or a specially powerful verse, will be more acceptable to the god than butter or honey. Therefore men honour the gods as frequently as they can; to them, the mighty ones above, they pray at early morning, at midday, and at the setting of the sun, for wealth and happiness, for health and long life, for a hundred autumns without the burdens of old age, which causes the beauty of the form to disappear like mist; for the blessing of offspring and an honourable position among friends and the whole people; for protection against all dangers and adversaries, at home and abroad; for victory and rich booty from every enemy, Aryan and barbarian. "Grant me," cries Gṛtsamada to Indra,—

"Grant me, O God, the highest, best of treasures,
A judging mind, prosperity abiding,
Riches abundant, lasting health of body,
The grace of eloquence, and days propitious".

—2. 21. 6.

And others in the people pray to the Highest, to "the gods, bright and clear as a spring, superior to blemish, deceit, and harm," that to their former benefactions they may add the protection which frees even the guilt-laden from his guilt, like the captive from his bonds; "for every one," cries a singer, "returning from his sins, you wisest gods, make live again." They are besought from guilt incurred or unaccomplished to guide to well-being and to protect from sins great and small. Man hopes that in the presence of these pure ones he shall again see his father and mother, and be united with his ancestors who have gone before.

Beside this purer conception, which regards the gifts of sacrifice as the free-will offerings of a heart filled with thankfulness, though perhaps hoping too for new aid, the calculating spirit, here as elsewhere, shows itself from the very beginning, which regards the god as under obligation for the gifts, and permits the sacrificer to expect, or almost to demand, a gift in return. "I give to thee,—do thou give to me," is the keynote of many hymns; and many a singer declares that only the songs and sacrifices, and above all the Soma, first gave the gods the courage and power for their saving deeds of might. But when once such results were confidently awaited from such gifts, it was only a step to the further conclusion that these deeds of the gods had been made possible only by the men's gifts, and that the gods were therefore dependent upon the acts and will of men, especially of those men who were familiar with the ancient songs and the conduct of the sacrifice,—the priests. In their hands remained the knowledge of the hymns and the ritual connected with them, while the mass of the people had in general far too much to do in waging war against the aborigines to be able to occupy themselves with other matters; all their energy was employed in maintaining their position and conquering new homes. In the strange land, where the customs of home are always invested with a sacred charm, the guardians of the old worship came more and more into the foreground. A creation and at the same time a personification of priestly action is seen in Bṛhaspati or Brahmaṇaspati, *i.e.*, the Lord of Devotion. To him are ascribed by later singers the deeds for which formerly other gods, notably Indra, were celebrated, and in very many old hymns interpolations and additions are plainly recognizable for the purpose of confirming the superiority of the human lords of prayer, the priests, over all the other classes, because only they knew how to present the effectual song and sacrifice, and therefore alone could secure the aid of the gods. Even in the second period of Vedic literature, in the Brâhmaṇa, we read that "there are two kinds of gods, the *devas* and the *brâhmaṇas* (*i.e.*, the priests), who are to be held as gods among men." "The wise Brahmana has the gods in his power," etc. Such a conception is naturally foreign to the old hymns; on the other hand, even then success and a continuance of prosperity seem to have led to a denial of gods who ordered all things with strong hand. "The sun and moon in turn fulfill their course, that man may look and believe in God," but the people living in prosperity does not heed this. "Nowhere, Indra," cries a singer, "canst thou find a rich man for thy friend; men insolent from drinking hate thee; but when thou thunderest loud, thou bringest them together: then as a father thou art called upon". "When he hurls hither and thither his lighting, then they believe on the gleaming god."

THE VEDIC BELIEF

The individual gods, corresponding to their origin from the personification of natural phenomena, are depicted as supreme in their own spheres, and in the Rigveda a younger race of gods stands plainly in the foreground. The old Father of Heaven, Dyaus (Zeus, Diespiter, Tyr, Zio), the divine parents, Heaven and Earth (Dyâvâpṛthivî), Trita and others have almost entirely disappeared and have been superseded by new forms, the representatives of those phenomena which in their new homes made a specially vivid impression on the minds of the Aryans, or exercised a special influence on their manner of life. Thus in one tribe we find one god pre-eminently reverenced, in another, another. And since there are many phenomena, and hence many gods, we are at first impelled to designate the Vedic religion as polytheism; . it is not, however, polytheism in the usual sense, but it presents to us throughout a stage of religious thought which, elsewhere hardly observed, in India developed partly into monotheistic, partly into polytheistic conceptions, and which Max Muller has proposed to designate by the name Henotheism or Kathenotheism;—a belief in single gods, each in turn standing out as the highest. And since the gods are thought of as specially ruling in their own spheres, the singers, in their special concerns and desires, call most of all on that god to whom they ascribe the most power in the matter,—in whose department, if I may say so, their wish comes. This god alone is present to the mind of the suppliant; with him for the time being is associated everything that can be said of a divine being;—he is the highest, the only god, before whom all others disappear, there being in this, however, no offence or depreciation of any other god.

Since that which was told of one god could so easily be spoken of others, it was natural to combine individual related gods, possessing certain qualities or rights in common, into dual divinities. Thus Indra (the conqueror of every enemy) and Agni (the conqueror of darkness and the dark hostile demons), the two lords, "Indra, the hero, and Varuna, the king," Indra and Vâyu, Rudra and Soma, and others, are praised and reverenced together. Later on the composers of a large number of hymns sought to win a unified expression for the numerous individual gods by grouping them together under the comprehensive name of *viśve devâ, i.e., all gods.* Others distinguish older and newer gods whom they try to systematize, or declare openly that a given god is identical with several others, and show in this an inclination toward a monotheistic conception, which will occupy us later on in the philosophical poetry.

THE GODS

Passing on to the consideration of the individual gods, I remark that I do not propose to give a complete Vedic mythology, examining all the mythological representations contained in the Veda with respect to their origin, history, chronology and order;[23] but on the other hand, I have been careful to collect all the essential characteristics given in the hymns into a general view of each divinity. In this I have confined myself as closely as possible to the words of the hymns, so that the whole work is, so to speak, made up of the words of the poets themselves. The metrical citations are for the greater part taken from *Siebenzig Hymnen des Rigveda*,[24] which give the reader a general view of the poetry of the Rigveda.

In the classification of gods I follow a very old division of the universe, contained in the hymns themselves, into the three realms of the Earth, the Air and the bright Heaven. The basis of this threefold division is the separation of air and light. The realm of light is not in the air-region, but beyond it, in the infinite space of the heaven; it is not confined to the shining mass of the sun, but is an independent, eternal force. Between this world of light and the earth lies the region of the air, which is under the control of gods, in order to keep the path of the light to earth unobstructed, to give passage to its enlivening force, and at the same time to allow the heavenly waters, whose home is also in the light region, to fall on the fields of the earth.

The Earth was given by the gods to men for a

dwelling-place. But aside from the fact that all the gods, in heaven and on earth, everywhere reveal their power in the waters, herbs and trees, and have implanted Will in man's body, they have chosen a representative from their midst to dwell here, among mortals immortal. Like a loving friend they have placed in the dwellings of men **Agni**, the god of fire. Born from the floods of heaven (the clouds), he first came down to earth as lightning, and when he had disappeared and remained hidden, Mâtariśvan, a demi-god, another Prometheus, brought him back again from afar from the gods to men, to the tribe of Bhṛgus. From that time the latter have been able to create him anew for themselves; in a multitude of hymns and innumerable images is sung his production from two sticks rubbed together,—his "parents." He lies concealed in the softer wood, as in a chamber, until, called forth by the rubbing in the early morning hour, he suddenly springs forth in gleaming brightness. The sacrificer takes and lays him on the wood; greedily he stretches out his sharp tongue and melts the wood. When the priests pour melted butter upon him, he leaps up crackling and neighing like a horse,—he whom men love to see increasing like their own prosperity. They wonder at him, when, decking himself with changing colours like a suitor, equally beautiful on all sides, he presents to all sides his front.

"All-searching is his beam, the gleaming of his light,
His, the all-beautiful, of beauteous face and glance,
The changing shimmer like that floats upon the stream,
So Agni's rays gleam ever bright and never cease."

—I. 143. 3.

Although the first of the gods, he is yet, because every morning kindled anew, the youngest; gleaming with brightness he whirls upward the sacred, light-red smoke; growing from his flames, which never age, from himself, he mounts on high, sweeps the heavenly vault with his flowing locks, and mingles himself with the sun-beams. Then they offer to him prayer and song, the devout sacrificial gift, that he may carry it on his gleaming chariot to the Immortals; or he can bring down the gods, ready to give aid, to the pious worship of men, to the drinking of the Soma at the sacred place of sacrifice; for gods and men have chosen him, who rules over heavenly as well as earthly things, for their messenger, the sacrificial carrier. Once, it is said, he was weary of the service, so that he refused longer to fulfil the office; from Varuṇa, who tries to persuade him, he demands remuneration for his labour:.

> "Then give me all the first and last libation,
> And give the juciest sacrificial portion,—
> The cream of water and the herbs' aroma,
> And long, O Gods, shall Agni's life continue".
>
> —10. 51. 8.

As Varuṇa grants all this, Agni yields and remains thereafter the High Priest of men, who above all knows the sacred institutions and times. If at any time men unknowingly transgress the laws of the knowing (gods), or if in foolishness mortals, weak in discernment, neglect the sacrifice, he, the best sacrificer, makes everything right. And when the light of day, the sun, has departed, Agni is visible through the darkness of night, and by this divine power he proves himself the victorious conqueror of gloom and its evil spirits, the ghosts and goblins, the magicians and witches. So the god becomes a visible saviour, a strong fortress for the devout. He drives away the noxious tribes from their dwelling-places, he burns them down like dry bushes, and the Immortal, bringing joy to mortals, finds a home in their midst. He orders their hosts and protects their settlements; from fear of him, whom the gods placed as a light to the Aryans, the black tribes fled; scattering, they abandoned their possessions, and the god breaks their strongholds. He overthrows barbarian and Aryan enemies, and sweeps away their wealth from field and mountain. In him, the lord of riches, lies all wealth, as the rays lie hid in the sun; like a king he protects all treasures, whether they are contained in the mountains, in the plants, in the waters, or among men. From him proceed all gifts of fortune, as branches from the tree, and to him are directed the thoughts of the devout as man's eyes turn to the sun. He may be looked upon as father and relation, dear friend and brother; called upon and reverenced, he brings with bounteous hands rich wealth into the house of the highly-favoured singer. Therefore he is a welcome guest to all men, and in every place a beloved family friend.

GENII OF THE SEASONS

In the middle realm of the **Air**, various divinities of the wind and storm are supposed to live, as well as the genii of the seasons, the **Ṛbhus**. These three skilful men by their dexterity gained divine honours, a share in the sacrifice and immortality. Since they made the chariot of the Asvins, the daily course of these gods, bringing blessing to man, is their deed; by them too were formed Brhaspati's miraculous cow and Indra's obedient team, which harness themselves at his command. They cherished and cared for their parents, long since broken down by age, with miraculous powers, until their youthful vigour returned; and many other wonderful deeds they accomplished on their journey, until they were received as guests in Agohya's house.[25] Here they spend twelve days in enjoyment; then the course begins anew, and anew the earth brings forth fruit, the streams flow; plants cover the heights, and waters the depths. Impressed by all these things, the gods wish to try their skill and send Agni as messenger to commission the Rbhus to fashion, from the one cup of the gods, the masterpiece of the gods' workman Tvashṭar, four others like it. They at once accomplish the work and more, so that Tvashṭar, overcome by jealousy, hides himself. But the gods rejoice in the work, looking at it with understanding and appreciation; and they search everywhere for the Rbhus and lead them to the company of the gods, where they find the reward of their zeal.

VAYU THE WIND GOD

Vâta (Vâyu), the wind, first arises in the early morning to drink the Soma and leads in the dawn. Then all the winds follow him like maidens to the feast. His approach is perceived by the waving of the flame; he is recognized hastening along the paths of the air in his swift car, never stopping; but each one asks:

"In what place was he born, and from whence comes he?
The vital breath of gods, the world's great offspring,
The God where'er he will moves at his pleasure:
His rushing sound we hear—what his appearance, no one knows"
—10. 168. 3. 4.

Rudra, the god of the destroying storm, is loudly sung because he, most beautiful of those that were born, strongest of the strong, with the lightning in his hands from his high seat looks out upon the inhabitants of the earth and the heavenly race. Where he sees a wrong, there he casts his mighty spear or sends a swift arrow from his strong bow and strikes the evil-doer. But he is glad to be called upon by the upright, who look for his coming as the child seeks his father's embrace. From them he wards off all affliction and hurt; purifying the air from all harmful miasmas, he furnishes to men and cattle the best nourishment; therefore he is called the very best of physicians.

"Let me through thy best medicines, O Rudra,
My life on earth prolong a hundred winters;
From us dispel all hatred and oppression,
On every site calamity drive from us.

Where then, O Rudra, is thy hand of mercy,
The hand that healing brings and softens sorrow,
That takes away the ills even which the gods send?
Let me, O mighty one, feel thy forgiveness.

The hero gladdened me amid the tumult
With greater might when I his aid entreated.
Like some cool shade from the sun's heat protected,
May I attain to Rudra's grace and refuge".

—2. 33. 2. 7. 6.

Rudra's sons and companions are the richly-adorned, well-armed **Maruts,** the gods of the thunder-storm, "the heavenly singers". Loudly thundering, they are visible far off as the stars of heaven and deck their forms like a prosperous wooer. On their heads golden helmets gleam, on their shoulders they carry gaily-coloured skins and spears, on their breasts golden breast-plates, about their ankles golden bracelets and clasps, in their hands gleaming, fire-darting weapons, and in their strong arms rich wealth for the worshipper. Now they set out with battle axe and spear, with bow and arrow, as the active and daring allies of Indra; again, they equip themselves for battle alone, rushing forth in golden chariot borne through the air untiringly by golden-hoofed horses or dappled mares. When they approach roaring and throw out their lines to measure the sun's path, when the rivers reverberate with the rumbling of their wheels,—when they raise their song of the storm-clouds and down upon the earth the lightnings smite,—then both men and the mighty, lofty mountains are terrified; the heavenly canopy trembles at their raging, the immovable rocks quake, the earth is moved, and like elephants the heroes destroy the forests; the mountains yield to their coming and the streams to their command. Even in bright day-time they make darkness when they shake down the milk of the clouds, or when they summon the rain-god **Parjanya**. Like as a driver whips and urges his horse, he rouses up his rain-messengers with wild uproar, deep as the distant roar of the lion. Swiftly Parjanya collects his clouds for rain; the winds rush, the lightnings fall stroke on stroke, with which the mighty one smites the blasphemer and terrifies even the pure; the heaven strains and swells; then at once the floods rush down,

> "And every creature then receives the quickening draught,
> When o'er the land Parjanya's grateful stream descends.
>
> The thirsty fields he covered with the waters,
> Of plenteous falling rains; but 'tis enough now.
> He caused the herbs to spring for our refreshment,
> And what his people sought of him has granted".
>
> —5. 83. 4. 10.

But the chief figure in the air-space is **Indra,** the most celebrated god of the Vedic period. During this time he assumes a more and more dominating position, and becomes the real national god of the Indians. In numberless hymns his deeds are celebrated, above all his conquest of the demons, Vṛtra ("surrounder"), Ahi ("confiner"), Sushṇa ("parcher") and others, who in the form of mighty serpents or dragons, encompass the waters and shut off their path, as well as that of the light, from the heights of heaven to man's earth. The ever-recurring celebrations of this victory are often tiresome but their explanation is found in the climatic conditions of the land. These descriptions and images, as, *e.g.*, John Muir, the accomplished investigator assures us, are perfectly natural and easy of comprehension, especially for those who lived in India and witnessed the phenomena of the various seasons there. He says:

"The growth of much of the imagery thus described is perfectly natural, and easily intelligible, particularly to persons who have lived in India, and witnessed the phenomena of the seasons in that country. At the close of the long hot weather, when every one is longing for rain to moisten the earth and cool the atmosphere, it is often extremely tantalizing to see the clouds collecting and floating across the sky day after day, without discharging their contents. And in the early ages, when the Vedic hymns were composed, it was an idea quite in consonance with the other general conceptions which their authors entertained, to imagine that some malignant influence was at work in the atmosphere to prevent the fall of the showers, of which their parched fields stood so much in need. It was but a step further to personify both this hostile power and the beneficent agency by which it was at length overcome. Indra is thus at once a terrible warrior and a gracious friend, a god whose shafts deal destruction to his enemies, while they bring deliverance and prosperity to his worshippers. The phenomena of thunder and lightning almost inevitably suggest the idea of a conflict between opposing forces; even we ourselves, in our more prosaic age, often speak of the war or strife of the elements. The other appearances of the sky, too, would afford abundant materials for poetical imagery. The worshipper would at one time transform the fantastic shapes of the clouds into the chariots and horses of his god, and at another time would seem to perceive in their piled-up masses the cities and castles which he was advancing to overthrow". (Muir O. S. T. 5. 98).

The heavens themselves, the songs say, shrink back at the roaring of the dragons; even the gods, all of them Indra's friends, at Vṛtra's snorting leave their champion to his fate, and the young hero's mother is concerned for him. But he, inspired by the songs of his adorers, strengthened by deep draughts of Soma and rich sacrificial gifts, armed with the thunder-bolt, which Tvashṭar made for him, advances boldly with his companions, the warlike Maruts; he encompasses the Encompasser; him, relying on his wiles, fighting without hands or feet against Indra, he overpowers by his craft, striking him in the face and back with his swift lightning; he finds the vulnerable parts of him who thought himself invulnerable, and with mighty blows smites the lurking encompasser of the waters. Like the branch hewn off by the axe, Ahi lies prone on the earth; and over his body the mighty waves rush joyfully; while Indra's enemy sinks into lasting darkness, the god, the Thunderer, brings the sun to believing mortals.

At another time the fight goes thus. The gods have

all declined on account of old age and put him forward as the only strong one, giving over to him all their power and intelligence; even the Maruts, who on other occasions remain true, stay behind. The demon shatters the god's cheek; but he, though wounded, soon masters the enemy; as soon as Indra becomes really earnest in his wrath, he who believed himself alone unconquerable, who considered himself a little god and immortal, finds a mightier, who does not yield in defiance even to the Defiant, whose might no one has attained, now or formerly. He whets his thunderbolt like a sharp knife on the rock, and the weapon rings loud when man's friend strikes down man's enemy, like the oak struck by the lightning, 'on wide meadow shortening the demon's days'. The foaming of the waters rushing forth carries away the demon's head; then the god first holds the floods together, that they may not (unnecessarily) flow asunder, but afterward lets them run freely in streams and sets the sun in the heavens. The victor, into whose own heart fear has crept at the thought of the avenger of the evil, receives the god's jubilations; the wives of the gods bring him a song of praise; mortals praise him with music and song and at their feasts loudly celebrate the Mighty's mighty deeds.

In another account the story tells that the Paṇis (the avaricious ones) have driven off the rainclouds, pictured as herds of cows, and are keeping them in the caves of the rocks. To them comes Indra's messenger Saramâ, to demand the return of the stolen herds. When they defiantly mocking ask:

"Who is he? What does he look like, this Indra,
Whose herald you have hastened such a distance?
Let him come here, we'll strike a friendship with him;
He can become the herdsman of our cattle,"

Saramâ answers warningly:

"Ye cannot injure him; but he can injure,
Whose herald I have hastened such a distance.
Deep rivers cannot cover him nor hide him;
Ye Paṇis soon shall lie cut down by Indra!"

—10. 108. 3. 4.

In vain;—trusting in their sharp weapons they remain defiant: "You have come to no purpose; nothing is to be found here." But now, united with the Angiras[26] the mighty god draws near, at whose breath both worlds tremble. He drives asunder the mountain strongholds and sweeps away the cunningly built walls. Fearing his blow the cavern opens and from its depths Indra drives forth the herds on pleasant ways; as the trees grieve over their plumage (foliage) stolen by the cold, so Vala (the cave-demon) laments the stolen cattle.

And in the mighty strife of the elements he is always victor:

"When heaven and earth together join in battle,
Marshalled by thee, like men that call upon thee,—
For surely thou wert born to might and power,—
Thou active dost destroy the slothful demon".

—7. 28. 3.

The immovable, too, he moves, and shakes everything that is to its deepest foundation; even the mighty mountains from fear of him are moved like atoms:

"Through fear of thee upon the earth is shaken
E'en the immovable,—the ether,—all things,
The earth, the heavens, mountains, forests tremble;
The firm foundation trembles at thy going."

—6. 31. 2.

But he calms them all again; he hews down the summits of the mountains; demons stealthily climbing up, seeking to mount up to heaven, he shakes off and thrusts them back. He steadies the trembling earth and brings the staggering mountains to rest; at his command they stand fast; the great heaven bows in reverence to Indra and this earth to his might.

Indra is thus a god of battle, the ideal of an ever-fighting, never conquered hero, and, therefore, the favourite of the race fighting for new homes and rich herds; for, as in the battle with Vṛtra all power was yielded to him, so in subduing men, lordship and victory were given him by the gods.

The man who trusts him in the decisive hour carries off the spoils of victory: in him the Aryan has found an ally able to contend with the barbarians, who overthrows fifty thousand of the dark race, and casts down their strongholds as the cloak slips from the shoulders of old age. Men seek to draw the "son of mighty deeds", near with the most pleasing song, the richest sacrifice, and the strongest draughts of Soma. For he is no friend or companion of the man who provides no Soma, and has no favour for the rich miser who grudges gifts; but gladly he enters the house where the sacrificial straw is prepared for him, where songs rise to heaven, and the Soma is cheerfully pressed, and where the god is sought with the whole heart. Such a man's herds he never allows to perish; for the sacrificing hero he secures freedom, and plenteous riches for the singer who praises him.

On him all men must call amid the battle;
He, high-adored, alone has power to succour.
The man who offers him his payers, libations,
Him Indra's arm helps forward in his goings.

They cry aloud to him amid the contest,
Rushing to deadly combat, to protect them,
When freind and foe lay down their loves in warfare,
In strife to conquer peace for child and grandchild.

They gird themselves, O Mighty, for the conflict,
Provoking each the other to the quarrel;
And when the hostile armies stand opposing,
Then each would have great Indra for his ally.

Then their oblations all they bring to Indra,
And freely then the meats and cakes are offered;
Then they who grudged before come rich with Soma,—
Yea, they resolve to sacrifice a bullock.

Yet still the god gives him success who truly
With willing mind pours out the draught he longs for,
With his whole heart, nor feels regret in giving;—
To him great Indra joins himself in battle.

4. 24. 2—6

So he allied himself with the Indian race in their expedition and conquered their enemies; he alone subdued the nations under the Aryans and gave them the land; the barbarians he put aside to the left, gaining far-spread brightness (great happiness) for the Aryan, and increasing his power, so that he can lead his enemies hither and thither at pleasure. He turned the broad-spreading floods into an easily passable ford for Sudâs. the pious Tṛtsu King, and, in the battle of the ten kings, rescued him from the onslaughts of innumerable enemies. With Suśravas, who was without allies, he crushed with fatal chariot wheel twice ten chieftains and their 60,099 warriors.

"The mighty stream, with flood o'erwhelming all things,
Thou heldest back for Vâyya and Turvîti;
Obedient stood the rapid flood, O Indra,
And through its bed thou mad'st an easy pathway".
—4. 19. 6.

And Indra restrained the waters also for Yadu and Turvaśa when they desired to cross the stream; and even all the gods could not withstand Indra when he prolonged day into the night, and the sun unharnessed his chariot in the midst of heaven (day).

From these acts men grew to see in him the creator and sustainer of the world, the leader of the races of men and gods, the mighty unrestricted lord and master, the harsh punisher of the godless, and the unfailing shield of the righteous. He made the heaven, the sun and the dawn and the earth as a likeness of heaven; he placed bounds to the air and pillars to the heavens; like two wheels upon one axle he set heaven and earth apart, and fixed them both. He placed the moon in the sky, he bids the sun traverse the wide space, and brings it to rest when it has finished its course. He created the matchless lightning of heaven, and the cloudy vault around; on earth, he divided the brooks according to their order, and in the field the plants bearing flowers and those with fruits; relying on him, the farmer puts his hand to the sickle. From him come right thoughts, and every good intention in man; he is the king of the worlds and peoples, seeing and hearing all; he leads the human and divine hosts, and none equals him;—how should any surpass him?

The poets never tire of praising his greatness and

might; one doubts whether before him wise men ever reached the whole of all Indra's greatness, and another, rescued from great need, declares that he does not know the whole greatness of the god, the might of the mighty one, and that no one comprehends the divine power of his present favour. He overtops both heaven and earth; both together cannot reach his greatness; the air, and the depths of the sea, the winds and the ends of the earth cannot contain him. Indra rejoices far out beyond stream and land. Both worlds (earth and heaven) form ideas of his sublimity, but they cannot comprehend it; his half equals both of them; when he grasps both these unbounded worlds together, they are but a handful; as a skin his power rolls heaven and earth together; they both roll after him (by the necessity of nature) as the wheel after the horse. His days do not pass in human fashion; neither years nor moons make him old; the course of days do not cause him to fade, and when he thinks, "I shall not die," with him even this remains true. Not the heavens can restrain his, the Mighty's, might; not days, not years, not moons:, the work the hero sets about he accomplishes, and no one is able to hinder him. To-day he performs one act, to-morrow another; he calls that which does not exist into being, and even through weakness accomplishes wonderful deeds. In his two hands he holds the nations and their possessions; he causes their hosts to war and again leads them to peace; he animates the spirit of heroes in battle against their enemies, though unnoticed by the wise and by the hosts, numerous as the stars. He gives over the great into the hand of the small; those who think themselves great he entangles in battle, and is the subduer of the haughty. The powerful one hurls aside the proud fool; the Mighty overthrows him who decks his body, who joins himself to the niggardly, and trusts in his own arm. One he makes homeless, to another he gives a home; as a man puts his feet in turn one before the other, he makes the first last; he breaks friendship with the former, joins himself in turn to the latter, and shakes off those who are not devoted to him.

> "The hero—listen—overcomes the mighty,
> Now to the front brings one and now another;
> The lord of both the worlds hates all the haughty,
> He cares for those who feel themselves but human."
>
> —6. 47. 16.

All those who are guilty of great crime he strikes with his arrow when they least expect it, and smites down every one who does not keep his promise, who perverts the truth, the scheming, foolish mocker. The rich man, who presses no Soma for him, he drags forth from his concealment, unsummoned he destroys the haters of prayer; he disperses the assemblies of the unsacrificing on all sides; even in unapproachable strongholds those who have enkindled his wrath, all together cannot withstand his strength. For them there is no help if they turn to the god in the day of need and promise him the richest gifts.

> "I never knew a man to speak so to me,
> When all the enemies are safely conquered;
> Yea, when they see how fierce the battle rages,
> They even promise me a pair of bullocks.
>
> When I am absent far in distant places,
> Then all with open hand their gifts would bring me;
> I'll make the wealthy niggard needy,
> Seize by the foot, and on the hard rock dash him."
>
> —10. 27. 3. 4.

But to the upright man, whose strength rests on Indra, who has never led another aside to godlessness, and has never knowingly neglected the god's songs; whose hope ever seeks the god anew, calling to him at morning and evening, by day and night; who from love toward him relinquishes his desire,—to him the world's lord offers riches with his left hand and is not doubtful with his right; to him he shows himself as his friend and saviour and liberator, as his present and future protector by day and night, as the pitying supplier of his needs, who wards off want and hunger and frees even from great guilt. The singer is dear to the god, who loves above all to listen to prayer; not the deep stream and not the lofty firm rock, no mortal and no god can hinder him when he desires to grant the upright man his desires, to give him protection and bestow rich herds upon him. Sometimes, indeed, he keeps his adorers in suspense, so that they anxiously ask when he will heed their words.

> "What now shall be with hymns thy fitting service?
> How shall we honour thee aright, O Indra?
> I bring in love to thee all my devotion;
> Hear therefore now, O Indra, this my crying."
>
> —7. 29. 3.

Then the sceptic scoffingly seeks to undermine the faith of the believer when he exerts himself in holy acts, asking him if the god has ever stood by him.

> "How then can Indra hear when men entreat him?
> How, if he hears, could he find means of succour?
> And where is all his wondrous consolation?
> How can men call him generous to the singer?

How does the man who serves him, even zealous
And full of piety, obtain his promised bounty?"
"The god be witness of my deeds' devotion,
My prayer receiving and rejoicing in it"[1]

—4. 23. 3. 4.

And when the man, now wavering in his trust, cries out:

"Lift up loud songs of praise to gain his favour,
Real praise to Indra, if there really be one.
'There is no Indra,' many men are saying;
'Who ever saw him? Why should we adore him?"

—then the god appears to him and speaks:

"I am, O singer, look on me, here am I,
And I am greater than all living creatures.
The service of the sacred rite delights me,
Destroying, I creation hurl to ruin."[2]

—8. 89. 3. 4.

So men seek more and more to win Indra for a friend, whether praising him in the dwelling of the singer or in the stillness with a song. Whoever strives to gain anything chooses Indra for an ally:

"The former, middle, latter call upon him,
On Indra, wanderers and the home-returning,
On Indra, those in peace and those in warfare,
On Indra, heroes striving after booty.

—4. 25. 8.

---

[1] *i.e.* let my devotion please the god, so that he may not let me come to shame before the mockers.

[2] He helps the devout, but destroys the godless.

The voice of all is:

"Praise the great praiseworthy Indra,
Ruler of the world, with singing,
Him the richest man, the victor.

Him let every creature honour,
Him in works and him in action;
Indra 'tis who brings us freedom.

All the mortals, all the peoples,
Ever in their hymns praise Indra,
Him in songs and him in measures.

Who to highest weal conducts us,
Lends success and fame in battle
And our foes subdues in conflict.

Carry us across as boatman,
Often praised, on ships to fortune,
Indra over every rival.

Help us, Indra, with refreshing,
Paths prepare us through thy goodness
And to happiness conduct us".

—8. 16. 1. 6. 9. 10-12.

ASVINS, THE HORSE-GUIDERS

Among the divinities of the light heaven we have first to mention the two **Asvins,** the "horse-guiders." These are the earliest light-bearers in the morning sky. As soon as the first beams shine in the east at break of day, the sacrifice is made ready for the two tons of heaven, two eternally young and beautiful heroes of miraculous power and deep wisdom. With uplifted hands the singer sends up his devout song of praise as a messenger to the twins, who overcome all darkness; he calls to these two helpers as a son to his parents. At their signal the golden sun-like chariot is harnessed, which stretches over all peoples, and with its wheels touches the ends of heaven and earth. The skilful Rbhus fashioned his chariot with three seats and three wheels; without horse and without bridle it glides sure and unwavering, as though on wings, to the house of the upright, bringing prosperity like a stream from the mountain; or, drawn by gold-winged steeds like eagles, it hastens daily with the speed of wind through all the regions of air, through sea and rivers, swift as thought,—swifter even than a mortal's thought, swifter than the twinkling of an eye. Toward the end of the night, the noble drivers mount the chariot, and with them Sûrya, the fair daughter of the Sun-god; she yielded herself to the beauteous heroes and chose both youths for husbands,—and all the gods assented from the heart. The journey begins; day and night divide; the limits of darkness gradually become visible; the Helpers approach from night and need, rich in joy and rich in wealth, the two guardians of treasure, with abundant, never-failing aid. As divine physicians they drive away sickness, bring medicines from far and near, and heal all that is hurtful; they give sight to the blind and make the lame walk; they help onward the outcast and the slow, even though left far behind. Like rotten cords they snap asunder the net of calamity, and at the feasts their deeds of wonder in the fathers' times are loudly praised among the people.

"Upon your chariot ye brought to Vimada
The daughter fair of Purumitra for his wife.
The eunuch's wife sent up her prayer to you,—ye came.
And made Puramdhi happily bring forth a child.

Ye gave to Kali, when he had grown old in years,
To him, the singer, all his youthful strength again;
And Vandana ye rescued from the deep abyss,
And quickly Viśpalā the maimed ye made to walk.

To Pedu ye, O Aśvins, gave the snowy steed,
The runner strong, whose ninety-nine fold wondrous strength
Bears on his rider in his flight; they cry to him
As to the goodness of a rich and kindly lord.

—10. 39. 7. 8. 10.

The wise Atri, through the wiles of a hostile monster, has fallen with all his host into a burning chasm; at his entreaty the Aśvins approach with eagle's speed, bringing a cooling and quickening draught; they protect him from the glowing flames, and finally lead him and his followers out to the life-giving air in full youthful strength. The Helpers took the body of the aged Cyavāna like a cloak, made it young and beautiful again, prolonged the life of the lonely one, and made him the husband of a young maiden. Rogues had kept Rebha hidden like a horse in the water, bound, wounded, overwhelmed by the flood; ten nights and nine days he lay there, till the Aśvins, with their wonder-working power, brought the dead forth and revived him. To the Pajrid Kakṣīvant they grant blessings in abundance; from the strong horse's hoof as from a sieve, they poured him forth a hundred jars of wine; and to Ghoṣā, remaining in her father's house, they gave a husband in her old age. The quail, seized by the wolf, they free from his jaws, and bring the sweet honey to the bees.

But among the many wonders for which they are

celebrated,—and there are very many,—none is sung so loud and so often as the rescue of Bhujyu, whom his father Tugra left behind, in the midst of the swelling waves, as a dead man abandons his possessions. Tossed about in the darkness he calls upon the youthful heroes, and they again are mindful of him, according to their wont, and hasten up with their red, flying steeds, self-harnessed, in their chariot, swift as thought. In the sea, which is without support, unceasing and unresting, they accomplish their heroic work: the struggling man is drawn into the hundred-oared craft, and the heroes, with miraculous power, bear the exile in the ship floating in mid-air to his home on the other side of the rolling sea, journeying three nights, and thrice by day. What wonder that every oppressed one longs for such helpers, who so often since the fathers' times, in every need, have stretched forth a saving hand, and that his desires look to them? As the wind drives the clouds, so the singer drives his songs of praise toward the lords of light; he calls upon them at home and on the journey; he seeks to attract them from far and near; from east and west, with the pleasing draught of milk; like buffaloes panting for the water's gleam, they are besought at milking-time, early in the day, at noon and at sunset, by day and night, to draw near the devout with blessing and support in his necessity. Since their former deeds never flag, they are both, for all time, the helpers of all men; ever regarding ancient friendships and relations, they ward off evil from their adorers, chase away hate and envy, lengthen their life, and overthrow their contemners. The man who reverences and praises them they bring to old age with seeing eye; they reward him with riches and the blessing of children, song for song, so that he enters into old age as into his own house.

After these much-praised lords of light, the Aśvins, in the Far East, out of the darkness from the boundary of heaven and earth rises the friendly Ushas, the dawn, the golden daughter of heaven, with kindly countenance, to show herself to the dwellings of men.[27] The two sisters, Night and Dawn, are unlike in colour, but of harmonious mind; in fixed succession they follow each other in daily interchange; as soon as the dark sister describes the light, she willingly gives place to her. Now, the fairest light of lights puts to flight the darkness of the night with its terrors; the pure goddess drives away haters and evil-doers. She makes the undesired darkness give way to sight, she opens the gates of heaven for every creature, and begins then to fill the wide spaces. White steeds, or bullocks, draw the well-adorned chariot of the goddess, self-yoking; in it she clears a goodly road and way first upon the mountains, then everywhere in the paths of men. She awakens all creatures,—only the miser must sleep on in the midst of darkness, without waking,—she brings renewed life and impels all things that live to motion; the winged flocks of birds fly forth; two-footed and four-footed creatures arouse themselves at her light; men take their morning meal and all the five peoples, whom daily she encircles, go forth to their occupations.

> "The goddess radiant bringing every splendour
> Appeared in light, and threw the portals open;
> All life arousing, she has shown us treasures,—
> The dawn has wakened every living creature.
>
> The sleeping man the goddess wakes to motion
> One to enjoyment, one to gathering treasure,
> The dim in sight to gaze afar about them,—
> The Dawn has wakened every living creature.

To lordship one, to win renown another,
One to get gain, one to his occupation,
Through all the various paths of life to journey,—
The Dawn has wakened every living creature".

—1. 113. 4-6.

Like a dancer the goddess puts on rich adornment; in all her form gleaming with fullness of beauty, like a maiden whom her mother has decked out, the radiant one with gracious smile displays her charms to the adorer, and brings rich treasure into the house of the man of upright mind: much life-sustaining wealth, in which the mortal rejoices, from which his fame grows wide among men.

Through two things, especially, this much-sung goddess awakened the astonishment of the Vedic singers. Knowing precisely the first sign of day, daily she accomplishes faultlessly her long journey, never transgressing the ordinance of the right and of the gods; skilfully she follows straight the path laid down, never failing in the direction, but appears day by day at the place appointed by the gods' commands. And when the singer sees these dawns come again and again, ever with the same beauty, old as time, yet eternally young, in appearance to-day alike, and alike to-morrow following the path of those preceding, at the same time the first of all that shall come after, then full of sadness he reflects:

"Vanished and gone long since are all the mortals
Who looked of old upon the dawn's bright radiance;
To-day she shows herself to us; and others
Shall come in future time to gaze upon her.

So oft before has goddess Ushas risen,
And now the rich one clothes the world with
glory,
And still in later days will gleam her brightness,
As pleases her, unaging, never-dying".
—1. 113. 11. 13.

"She comes in radiant colours, never fading,
And leads to age the life of every mortal;
Even as a gambler hides the dice with cunning,
So she removes the human generations".
—1. 92. 10. 11.

Then soon **Surya** himself, follows the sining goddess of the morning, as the youth the maiden's footsteps; the God-born light visible from afar, the son of heaven with golden hair, the Sun. Streaming forth in beams from the bosom of the dawn, the arouser of all men rises, saluted by the joyful exultation of the singers; he throws off the black cloak, his beams shake the darkness from him like a skin, and the stars with their gleam slink away like thieves.

"Whom they, whose home is fixed, their aim
unwavering,
Have made to drive away the hostile darkness,
The sun-god, all the ends of earth surveying,
By seven steeds, all light and swift. is carried.
—4. 13. 3.

The light and bright and beauteous steeds of
Surya,
The gleaming steeds, by songs of joy saluted,
They reverently climb the heights of heaven,
In one day all the realm of light traversing.
—I. 115. 3.

The golden ornament of heaven far-seeing,
Mounts, pressing to his distant goal, bright
gleaming.
Impelled by Sūrya's power, let all the mortals
Pursue their aims and carry on their labours.
—7. 63. 4.

So Sūrya rises every morning, an all-seeing searcher, mounts the high plains, looks down on right and wrong among men, guards the path of the upright, observes at bidding the occupation of each, and when at evening, his journey accomplished, he unharnesses his mares from the chariot, he commands to lay aside the work assigned in the morning, even though it be uncompleted; then Night spreads her veil over all. Unceasingly Sūrya's steeds carry now the bright gleam, now the dark, over the dome of the sky.

It is evident that the sun, this vital breath of animate and inanimate things, this bright divine countenance, imperishable in the heavens, prospering mankind without distinction,—this eye all-seen and all-seeing, which above all publishes the Immortals' might and wisdom, since it exalts them high in the heavens,—that the sun should be honoured and sung in a very special manner; and we find it variously displayed activity praised under various names.[28]

In **Pusan**, *i.e.*, 'Nourisher,' the great bringer of sustenance and lord rich in treasure is praised. As bestower of riches, making all men prosper, he also brings hidden treasure to light, compels the niggardly to give, and softens the heart of the miserly; he paves the way to gaining wealth, pierces the niggards' heart with his spear, and brings what was dear to them to his adorer.[29] Filling both the broad spaces, the flame-radiating god sits in the midst of heaven, and as shepherd of the world overlooks all creatures, accurately distinguishing them and surveying them all; as guardian of the herd, who governs animate and inanimate life, he weaves the sheep's dress and smoothes her coat; he follows the cattle and guards the steeds, that none of them may be lost or come to harm, none be dashed to pieces in the ravine, and that all may return unharmed.[30] As guardian of every road he clears and makes level the paths, goes before, sends on the skilful man and protects on every journey.[31] And since he knows the ways of heaven as well as earth and all the spaces, he goes before the souls of the dead on their journey to the abodes where the upright have gone, where they dwell.

The far-striding ruler of the heights, **Vishnu,** *i.e.*, the 'Worker,' is ever and anon praised for his great heroic deed, because he measured the whole wide earth in three strides, made supports for the kingdom on high and fastened the earth all about with pegs. His footprints are full of sweetness. a never-ceasing source of joy; he gave the vast expanse of earth with rich pastures to man for a sure dwelling-place. Two steps of the Sun-like we can recognise, though a mortal who would see them must diligently exert himself; but the third highest none dare apprach, not even the winged birds in their flight; it is known only to the Saviour full of mercy. Toward this highest footprint, placed like an eye in heaven, the wise ever look; there, at the spring of sweetness, the men devoted to the gods dwell in happiness.

Closely connected with Sûrya is **Savitar,** the 'Inciter, Inspirer, Enlivener'; the two words are, indeed, employed without distinction. But with Savitar the etymological meaning especially stands out clearly; the difference in the use of the names is usually this, that

Sûrya signifies more the sun-body, Savitar, the divine power behind it; *e.g.*, when we read,

> With golden hands comes hastening Savitar the god,
> Pursuing busily his work twixt heaven and earth;
> He drives away oppression, leads the sun-god forth;
> Through the dark realm of air he hastens up to heaven.—1. 35. 9.

Or, in another passage,

> The sun's uprising floods the air with brightness;
> God Savitar sends all men forth to labour, etc.
> —1. 24. 1.

Of Savitar it is described, in even more glowing colours than of Sûrya, how he with care and ceaselessly conducts day and night, defining their limits. Cunningly enveloped in the brilliancy of every colour, Savitar follows the path of Ushas; first the beloved god passes through this lower realm of air; enlivening, he stretches aloft his beauteous, slender golden arms, and, as he yesterday laid them to rest, to-day he awakens all creatures,—whatever has two feet or four, whatever is mortal and immortal,—to new life; man and beast must move again. With golden steeds in golden chariot he drives up the heights to the light world of the heavens and rests there, enjoying the brightness of the sun's beams. Wherever the faithful god appears with his golden radiance he drives away all oppression and brings contentment for man and beast. He sends infallible guardians about the house and home; he inspires courage, and with full hands brings rich store and comfort for man. Yet his best gift is that he awakens first immortality for the exalted gods, but for men, as their portion, life that follows life; he frees them from the guilt of sin and guides them to the resting-places of the blessed. So he blesses daily; in the morning he brings life and at evening rest; then he cloaks himself in brown-red mantle and hastens down the heights on well-paved, dustless paths; in the dark night, following his settled custom, Savitar guides the great host of stars.[32]

> The god his mighty hand, his arm outstretches
> In heaven above, and all things here obey him;
> To his commands the waters are attentive,
> And even the rushing wind subsides before him.
>
> Driving, his steeds, now he removes the harness,
> And bids the wanderer rest him from his journey,
> He checks the serpent-smiter's eager onset;
> At Savitar's command the kindly Night comes.
>
> The weaver roils her growing web together,
> And in the midst the workman leaves his labour;
> The god arises and divides the seasons,
> God Savitar appears, the never resting.
>
> In every place where mortals have their dwelling,
> The house-fire far and wide sheds forth its radiance.
> The mother gives her son the fairest portion.
> Because the god has given desire of eating.
>
> Now he returns who had gone forth for profit;
> For home the longing wanderer's heart is yearning;
> And each, his task half finished, homeward journeys.
> This is the heavenly Inciter's ordinance.
>
> The restless, darting fish, at fall of evening,
> Seeks where he may his refuge in the waters,
> His nest the egg-born seeks, their stall the cattle;
> Each in his place, the god divides the creatures.
>
> —2. 38. 2-6. 8.

The personifications of light already named, the Aśvins, Ushas, the Sun-gods, dwell in the highest realm, in the clear space of the heaven, but they are not the highest gods. Almost always their activity is pictured as bound to special phenomena, therefore confined to a relatively narrow sphere and not at all independent and unlimited. When Ushas each day intelligently appears at the right spot, she only follows higher laws, and when Savitar, like a spirited warrior swings high his banner, it is still Varuṇa and Mitra who, according to their decree, cause the sun to mount high in the heavens. While the poet praises Sûrya in inspired songs, he still knows that the divinity is only an instrument in the hands of higher powers,—that he is only the eyes of Varuṇa and Mitra; like an eagle soaring Sûrya follows the path where these immortals laid out the road for him. Therefore the libation and songs at sunrise are homage to Varuṇa and Mitra and Aryaman, the most celebrated among the Ādityas, the sons of Aditi.

To Aditi, 'eternity,' no hymns are directed; but she is often praised, as the friend of all men, the glorious, heavenly sustainer of the nations, the rich bestower of blessings, who gave life to Varuṇa and Mitra, the most mighty lords, as a revelation of the highest divine power. Men entreat her for sure protection and defence, and desire to be freed by her from the debt of sin.[33] But her sons, the seven Ādityas, are the absolute, the highest.

> "The gods, all light and clear as flowing fountains
> Uplifted above harm, deceit and blemish."—2. 27. 2.

From some of their names, in part of rare occurrence, one might be inclined to infer that, excepting Varuṇa, they had their origin not, as the other gods, in natural phenomena, but in moral ideas; but we have rather to see in them deep spiritual personifications of the heavenly light and its various developments. They, the righteous rulers, created the eternal order in the realm of nature as well as spirit, and they watch over it, that this their ancient ordinance of the world's government may ever have eternal continuance.[34] In the hymns to these 'living spirits of the gods' the religious feeling finds expression in the greatest depth, fervency and purity.

All the gods together chose these pure-minded, wise sons of wise parents for the highest divine power, and gladly gave over the dominion to them, so that they embrace both the wide worlds.

The Ādityas, through depth and breadth extending,
Unharmed by any, harming at their pleasure,
They, many-eyed, discern the straight and crooked;
For them all things are near, the furthest even.[35]

Inanimate and animate sustaining,
The heavenly guardians of the whole creation
Watch over their divinity, far-seeing;
Each evil deed with justice strict they punish.

No right or left, no back or front, Ādityas,
By mortal eyes in you can be distinguished.
No weariness can dim your eyes, nor slumber;
After your guardianship protects the upright.—2. 27.

Ever the pure ones, whose very breath suffices to hold the world in bounds, assert their dominion; as the unharmed, infalliable heads of the racts of men, they guard everywhere their firm decrees which no god dares to disturb, and woe to the mortal who should attempt to violate them. They see into the hearts of men and their thoughts, the false and those without deceit; to him who, clean from any sin, never practises what the good ones punish, the spotless sons of Aditi bring freedom out of need and oppression. They are his providers and his strength; when he trembles at danger and death, he flees for refuge to their heart; in them he finds protection and defence and comfort, and he entreats the infallible for their alliance. When he turns back from his sin, then they put far away the evil done openly or in serect, and prolong the life of the penitent. Although as man he is subject to death, yet the arrow of the death-god shall not strike him before a ripe old age, shall not hurry him away before his time in the midst of his work.

I pray for your protection, ye Ādityas,
I seek your strengthening power in hours of danger.
Led by your hand, Varuṇa-Mitra, may I
Escape for need as from a yawning chasm.

Your path is easy, Aryamaṇ and Mitra,
And thornless, Varuṇa, it leads straight onward.
On it, Adityas, lead us with your blessing.
And cover us with a defence enduring.

He dwells in peace in richly watered regions,
The pure one, rich in sons and armed with power.
No hostile weapons far or near, can reach him.
Who dwells defended by the great Ādityas.

Forgive, O Aditi, Varuṇa, Mitra,
If we in anyhting have sinned against you.
Let me attain the realms of peace and brightness,
Led by your hand, in folly or in wisdom.[1]

—2. 27.

[1] *i.e.*, let me enter the bright world of the blessed, who according to my powers now err, now do right.

The might and greatness of these eternal highest beings, their wisdom and justice, their sublimity and kindliness are united in the chief Aditya, VARUNA, originally the personification of the all-embracing heaven. In the preserved hymns he stands, compared with the national Indian god of battle, Indra, more in the background, and in many places the contrast appears prominently between the governing king of peace Varuṇa and the warlike martial hero Indra, loved and celebrated by the warlike nation; but the relatively few hymns to Varuṇa belong to the most exalted portions of the Veda. They recall especially the tone of the Psalms and the language of the Bible in general; to this point more attention will be directed hereafter. They picture the god as the all-wise creator, preserver and regent of the worlds, the omniscient protector of the good and avenger of the evil, holy and just, yet full of pity.

Like a cunning artist the all-wise god called all things, the heaven and the earth here, into existence. Through his might the broad, deep double realm of air stands fast; he propped the heavens and marked out the spaces of earth; as the butcher stretches a hide, he spread out the earth as a carpet for the sun, which itself he created in the heavens, a golden swinging light. He fills both worlds with his greatness, and bestows on every mortal that which gives him his value and worth.

> His works bear witness to his might and wisdom,
> Who fashioned firm supports for earth and heaven,
> Who set on high the firmament uplifted,
> And fixed the stars and spread out earth's expanses.
> —7. 86. 1.

He mingled with the clouds his cooling breezes,
He gave the cow her milk, the horse his spirit,
Put wisdom in the heart, in clouds the lightning,[1]
The sun in heaven, on the rock the Soma.—5. 85. 2.

The sun's sure courses Varuṇa appointed,
He sent the streaming waters flowing onward[2]
The mighty path of days he first created,
And rules them as the riders guide their horses.
—7. 87. 1.

Enveloped in golden cloak, in robes of glory, the lord of all stands in the air; with the cord he measured the ends of heaven and earth and with the sun as with a measuring staff he laid out the spaces of the earth, on which he places his mountains.

And the world which he created the lord of all life supports and carries; his breath blows as wind through the air, his eye, the sun, is the soul of the animate and inanimate; he gives drink to all creatures, as the rain to the fruits of the field. Sitting in his house with a thousand doors, he holds sway over the broad earth and high heaven, over gods and mortals, as absolute, unrivalled prince; in the foundations of the earth as in the air his dominion extends to the boundaries of the world, and nothing can withdraw itself from his sway. Immovably he protects his ancient, inviolable laws, his infrangible decrees in nature as well as in the life of men; for firmly on him as on a rock the ordinances are fixed eternally; for he is the omniscient ruler of all. He knows where the Pleiades, which show at night, go by day; he knows the secret hidden names of the dawn, the path of the

[1] *i.e.*, the lightning in the clouds.
[2] *i.e.*, since Varuṇa showed them the path.

birds that soar in the spaces of the air, the ships upon the sea, the twelve moons rich in children and the moon born after. Even the path of the wind, the gloriously mighty, and those who dwell beyond,—in short, every wonder, complete or to be completed, past and future, is revealed before him. And among man he looks upon right and wrong; he watches over the thoughts of mortals as the shepherd over his herds; yea, away from him and without him no one is master even of the winking of his eye.

It is admissible to insert here a fragment of the Atharvaveda, which gives expression to the divine omniscience more forcibly than any other hymn of the Vedic literature.

"As guardian, the Lord of worlds,
Sees all things as if near at hand.
In secret what 'tis thought to do
That to the gods is all displayed.

Whoever moves or stands, who glides in secret,
Who seeks a hiding-place, or hastens from it,
What thing two men may plan in secret council,
A third, King Varuṇa, perceives it also.

And all this earth King Varuṇa possesses,
His the remotest ends of yon broad heaven;
And both the seas in Varuna lie hidden,[1]
But yet the smallest water-drop contains him.

Although I climbed the furthest heaven, fleeing,
I should not there escape the monarch's power;
From heaven his spies descending hasten hither,
With all their thousand eyes the world surveying.

1. The "two seas" are the sea in the air and that on earth.

Whate'er exists between the earth and heaven,
Or both beyond, to Varuṇa lies open.
The winkings of each mortal eye he numbers,
He wields the universe, as dice a player".

—AV. 4. 16. 1-5.

Whoever here upon earth honours Varuṇa and submits willingly to his commands and his eternal ordinances, from him he takes away all anxiety and fear and spreads over him a threefold protecting roof; he is at hand with a hundred, a thousand remedies; he sharpens the courage and the understanding of the truly devoted,—the prayer which he himself inspired in his heart; even deep hidden secrets he imparts to the wise singer. With confidence the pious may look for his pity: the kind god gives him a hundred harvests and his desire joyful and pleasant old age,—and after death a new and blessed life united with the gods and his own people in the highest heaven.

But whoever, through any error, or any sin,[36] even without intention, offends against these eternal ordinances of the All-knowing, he arouses the anger of the Sinless, him messengers at the command of the Just punish, and bind him with the bonds of the god,—with calamity, with sickness and death.[37] No deceivers' deceit, nor the wily plans of man dare to approach the pure one: through reverence and prayer, through libation and sacrificial gifts every mortal seeks to allay the wrath of the Mighty. And the rigorous one is yet a god who pities the sinner and who therefore is the chosen recipient of prayer. To other gods men turn most for success and riches, for respect among the people and a numerous family, for victory and spoils; from Varuṇa is sought continually forgiveness of sin of every kind, since He has the power.

"If we to any dear and loved companion
Have evil done, to brother or to neighbour,
To our own countryman or to a stranger,
That sin do thou, O Varuṇa, forgive us."

—5. 85. 7.

"Forgive the wrongs committed by our fathers,
What we ourselves have sinned in mercy pardon;
My own misdeeds do thou, O god, take from me.
And for another's sin let me not suffer".

—7. 86. 5 and 2. 28. 9.

"If ever we deceived like cheating players,
If consciously we've erred, or all unconscious,
According to our sin do not thou punish;
Be thou the singer's guardian in thy wisdom."

—5. 85. 8 and 7. 88. 6.

The singer Vasiṣṭha is filled with pious grief, because daily, against his will and without knowledge, just as it often happens to men in their actions, he offends the god and in ignorance violates his decree. Full of woe, when the hand of the god lies heavy upon him, he recalls the time when, as his most intimate friend, he held close intercourse with the Lord, and had free approach to his high stronghold, the house of a thousand doors. Anxiously he searches after the heavy sin for which the just king now visits him, his constant, loving companion. Freed from sin he yearns to be permitted, full of reverence, to approach the merciful one, and he consults the wise men by day and in the night season. But from others he hears only what he has already discovered; that Varuṇa does not refuse his pity to him who in dire need calls upon him.

This thing by day, the same by night they tell me,
And this my own heart's voice is ever saying:
He, to whom cried the fettered Śunahśepa,
Great Varuṇa the king shall give us freedom.

For Śunahśepa once, bound to three pillars,
Called in his chains on Āditya for succour,
Let Varuṇa the monarch free me also,
He can,—and may the true one loose the fetters.

We turn aside thy anger with our offerings,
O king, by our libations and devotion.
Do thou, who hast the power, wise king eternal,
Release us from the sins we have committed.

—1. 24. 12-14.

And so the oppressed man calls and cries to him, the pitiful, in mercy to release him from all the guilt of sin; upon the heart of the god he presses his song, in which, full of childlike trust, he vows:

Thee I will follow, jealous god, and serve thee,
Faithful and true, as slaves a kindly master.
The god gives light to minds devout though simple,
The wise a wiser one conducts to blessing.

—7. 86. 7.

With Varuṇa is connected also the belief in personal immortality, in the life of the soul after death, "that real *sine qua non* of all true religion". That life is here understood throughout as the free gift of the gods, which they grant to every upright adorer. The dead body was either consigned to the flames or laid away to gentle rest in the mother earth. The earth-born shell is given back; it takes possession of its home in the broad bosom of the earth; but the soul of the pious man, which springs from above, cannot remain in the grave; another place has been found for it by the righteous forefeathers of olden times. Vivasvant's son, Yama, the first man, has gone to the distant heights, and has searched out a way to the 'world of the just' for the multitude after him.

> He went before and found a dwelling for us,
> A place from which no power can ever bar us.
> Whither our fathers all long since have journeyed;
> His path leads every earth-born mortal thither.
>
> —10. 14. 2.

Therefore, whether the flames devour the body or the earth covers it, the spirit, freed from all needs, moves through the air toward new life; led by Pūshan, it crosses the stream and passes by Yama's watchful dogs to the world of spirits from which it came.[38] "Go forth, go forth,"—so one hymn cries to the soul of the departed at the funeral ceremony:

> Go forth, go forth upon the path so ancient,
> By which our fathers reached their home in heaven.
> There Varuṇa shalt thou behold, and Yama,
> The princes both, in blessedness eternal.
>
> The spotted dogs of Saramā, the four-eyed,
> Pass calmly by and hold thy way straight onward;
> Enter the band of the propitious fathers,[1]
> Dwelling in blest abodes in bliss with Yama.
>
> Join thou thyself to Yama and the fathers;
> Meet there with thy reward in highest heaven;
> Return to home, free from all imperfection;
> In radiant power gain union with thy body.
>
> —10. 14. 7. 10. 8.

---

1. "Fathers" is here the standing epithet for the "blessed", the souls of the departed pious ones.

In the highest heaven, therefore, is the place, in Yama's bright realm,

> Where men devout in blessedness are dwelling,
> Where life to life succeeds for righteous spirits,
> And each is fuller than the last in beauty.
>
> —I. 154. 5.

There in the inmost midst of the highest heaven beams unfading light, and those eternal waters spring; there wish and desire and yearning are stilled; there dwell bliss, delight, joy and happiness. This life of bliss is not pictured more clearly in the hymns of the Rig; it is not asked how the new body will be endowed in that spirit-world, and whether new tasks await it there; the man strives only, living according to the commands of Varuṇa, to be guiltless before him and Aditi, and hopes in child-like confiding trust that he shall at some time live above in eternal light, united with his ancestors, with his father and mother, as a divine spirit among the blessed gods; that, like them in appearance and might, he may be their companion and helper in their works.

As to the eternal gods, so also reverence is shown to all who have passed away, the earlier, middle and last. When a man dies, or when the anniversary of a relative's death is celebrated, then with Yama and Agni all the fathers who are known and who are not known are summoned to the funeral feast, to the food on the sacrificial straw and to the prized Soma. And these who have become immortal look down upon mortals; these spirits of the dead care faithfully for their children here on earth. They move through the circle of the earth's atmosphere, through all the space of the air, among the races that dwell in beautiful villages, where men prepare the sacrifice and call them, there the holy, true, wise fathers come, full of gifts, with succour rich in blessing, with prosperity and blessing to the mortal adorer. They bring their sons might and wealth and posterity; they hear, help, comfort; they fight boldly like heroes in battle, they give a thousandfold reward for the offerings and punishment for wrong, if ever in human fashion mortals sin against them; for, themselves just, they rejoice in the right and preserve right and the divine ordinances of the Eternals. They lead the dawn across the sky, and with a thousand means and ways guard the sun; they deck the heavens with stars, as a dark stead with pearls, and lay darkness in the night, and in the day the light's radiance.

But to the wicked, lying evil-doers, to perverse, godless men, who violate the firm decrees of Varuṇa and Mitra, the ever watchful, to lustful, wicked women who hate their husbands, to all these that highest gift of the gods is denied; they remain shut out from the companionship of the immortals and the spirit-life in eternal light. As their bodies are sunk in the tomb, so their souls are cast into the pit, into deepest, hopeless darkness. Of the descriptions of the place of torment, as the phantasy of the later Indians and other peoples evolved them, the Rigveda knows as little as of the gloomy doctrine of metempsychosis, which afterwards fettered the spirits of India in chains.

Two gods yet remain to be mentioned, to each of whom in time the qualities and deeds of the other gods collectively were ascribed.

Soma was originally the sap pressed out form the swelling fibres of a plant. This herb, itself called Soma, was once brought by a fair-winged falcon from afar, from the highest heaven, or from the mountains, where Varuṇa had placed it, the world's governor. Its sap, purified, mixed with milk or a decoction of barley, and left for some time for fermentation, showed intoxicating effects, and was the favourite drink of the Aryans, the soul and adornment of the sacrifice, the joy of men. It is drunk by the sick man as medicine at sunrise; partaking of it strengthens the limbs, preserves the legs from breaking, wards off all disease and lengthens life. Then need and trouble vanish away, pinching want is driven off and flees when the inspiring one lays hold of the mortal; the poor man, in the intoxication of the Soma, feels himself rich; the draught impels the singer to lift his voice and inspires him for song; it gives the poet supernatural power, so that he feels himself immortal. On account of this inspiring power of the drink, there arose even in the Indo-Iranian period a personification of the sap as the god **Soma**, and ascription to him of almost all the deeds of other gods,[39] the strength of the gods even being increased by this draught. Like Agni, Soma causes his radiance to shine cheeringly in the waters; like Vāyu, he drives on with his steeds; like the Aśvins, he comes in haste with aid when summoned; like Pūshan, he excites reverence, watches over the herds, and leads by the shortest roads to success. Like Indra, as the sought-for ally, he overcomes all enemies, near and far, frees from the evil intentions of the envious, from danger and want, brings goodly riches from heaven, from earth and the air. Soma, too, makes the sun rise in the heavens, restores what has long been lost, has a thousand ways and means of help, heals all, blind and lame, chases away the black skin (the aborigines), and gives everything into the possession of the pious Ārya. In his, the world-ruler's, ordinance these lands stand; he, the bearer of heaven and the prop of earth, holds all peoples in his hand. Bright-shining as Mitra, awe-compelling as Aryaman, he exults and gleams like Sūrya; Varuṇa's commands are his commands; he, too, measures the earth's spaces, and built the vault of the heavens; like him, he too, full of wisdom, guards the community, watches over men even in hidden places, knows the most secret things. By Soma's side also, as by Varuṇa's, stand ready, never-sleeping scouts, his binding fetters follow at every step; he, too, is zealous to punish untruth and guilt. Therefore, to him, also, men pray to take away the wrath of the gods, to approach with good will and without anger, and mercifully to forgive every error of his adorer, as a father pardons his son.

King Soma, be thou gracious, make us prosper;
We are thy people only; know this surely.
Now rage and cunning lift their heads, O Soma;
Give us not over to our foes' desires.

Thou, Soma, guardian of our bodies, madest
Thy dwelling in each member, lord of heroes.
Though we transgress thy firm decree so often,
Be merciful to us, and kind and gracious.

—8. 48. 8. 9.

He will lengthen the life of the devout endlessly, and after death make him immortal in the place of the blessed, in the highest heaven.

It has already been remarked above, that **Bṛhaspati** or **Brahmaṇaspati**, the 'lord of prayer,' was 'a creation, and at the same time a personification of the priestly activity, to which later priestly poets ascribed the deeds of might for which formerly other gods, notably Indra, were praised'. Thus it is said of Bṛhaspati, that his prayer upheld the ends of the earth, he embraces the All; he split the rocks, took the strongholds, opened the cow-stalls and caused the floods to flow freely. All haters of devotion, despisers of the gods and enemies he exterminates, the stern avenger of crime; but on the man who believingly trusts in him he bestows victory and freedom, security and plentiful riches, youthful strength and a numerous family. He brings joy to the gods as well as to men; for only through his wisdom have the first obtained a share in the sacrifice; for the latter he created all prayers and makes them availing; he is their rightful, skilled priest and the Pontifex, the preparer of the way to the heights of heaven.

We must finally call attention to the fact that a not inconsiderable number of hymns is directed to "all gods". These are either each one in succession called by name and entreated, or the petitions are presented to them in a body; the adorer assures them that he neither secretly is guilty of many errors nor openly provokes their warth, and entreats of them imperishable prosperity.

We will here close our survey of the religious songs, and it remains to cast a glance at the not too numerous examples of **Secular Poetry**, if we may embrace under this title the songs not specially directed to divinities. We can naturally not look for a sharp division of the two chief groups; the transition from the first to the second is, perhaps, best formed by two hymns, which, belonging half to the religious, half to the secular poetry, are of the greatest interest for the history of civilization.

WEDDING-HYMN

The **Wedding-Hymn,** which, in the existing form is not a unit but a collection of marriage verses, relates first the wedding of the moon and sun, 'this prototype and ideal of all human weddings and marriages'. The two Aśvins present the suit of Soma to Savitar for the hand of his daughter, Sūryā, and he causes the bride heartily agreeing to be led to her husband's house. This wedding of Soma and Sūryā (i.e., of moon and sun) is pointed to as the pattern of married union in general to be followed. "As sun and moon ever support each other and alternate in their office, on the constant fulfilment of which depend not only the prosperity of all inanimate nature, but also the possibility of intercourse between men and the ordering of civil relations, even so man and wife must work together in harmony and with united powers untiringly fulfil the duties laid upon them in their vocation for the advancement of the family". The following quotations throw important light on the rites of marriage, which in the most essential traits agree with those of related peoples. When the relatives and acquaintances of the affianced pair are gathered in the house of the bride's parents, the fire is kindled on the house-altar and the bride is given over to the bridegroom by her father or his representative. With the formula—

> By thy right hand for happiness I take thee,
> That thou mayst reach old age with me, thy husband.
> Aryaman, Bhaga, Savitar, Puramdhi,
> Gave thee to me to rule our home together.
>
> —10. 85. 36.

the bridegroom with his right hand takes the right hand of the bride. He murmurs a number of traditional verses, as, *e.g.*, "I am he, thou art she; thou art she, I am he. Come, we two will go forth, we will beget us posterity, many sons will we get for us, they shall reach great age. In love united, strong, cheerful, may we see a hundred years, live a hundred years, hear a hundred years." Then he leads the bride solemnly three times from left to right around the altar. With this,—by the taking of the right hand and the leading about the altar, —the bride becomes legally a wife, the bridegroom her husband. After the wedding feast is finished, the wife, in her festal adornment, is transported to the new home on a wagon decked with flowers and drawn by two white steers. Here the newly-married couple are greeted with admonitions and good-wishes:

Here now remain, nor ever part;
Enjoy the whole expanse of life,
With son and grandson joyous sport,
Be glad in heart within your house.

Children and children's children grant, Prajāpati,[40]
Till hoary age may Aryaman preserve the bond.
From evil free enter thy husband's house and thine,
Within the home may man and beast increase and thrive.

Be free from evil looks and lack not wedded love,
Gentle in mind and face, bring e'en the beasts good luck;
Fearing the gods, do thou a race of heroes bear;
Within the home may man and beast increase and thrive.

In sons, O Indra, make her rich,
Give her a life of happiness;
Ten children grant, and spare to her
As an eleventh her dear spouse.

So rule and govern in thy home
Over thy husband's parents both;
His brother and his sister, too,
Are subject likewise there to thee.

—10. 85. 42—46

Another solemn occasion in the life of the Vedic people is presented in a **Funeral-Hymn.** The relatives and friends of the dead man, about to be buried, are assembled about the corpse which has been brought to the grave. By it the widow sits; the liturgy adjures death to depart, and summons those present to devotion.

Depart, O Death, and go thy way far from us,
Far from the path which by the gods is trodden.
Thou seest and hear'st the words to thee I utter;
Harm not our children, harm not thou our heroes.

Ye who have come here, blotting out Death's footprints,
And in your yet extended life rejoicing,
In wealth and children's blessing still increasing,
O reighteous men, your minds be pure and spotless.

—10. 18. 1. 2.

It then gives expression to the feeling of joy that the death-lot has not fallen to any of the assembly and urges all gladly to enjoy life in the future. A stone laid between those present and the dead typifies the separation of the realms of life and death; and in connection with it the wish is expressed that for all there a long life may be decreed.

The living from the dead are separated,
The sacred rite to-day has prospered for us,
And we are here, prepared for mirth and dancing,
Prolonging still the span of our existence.

This boundary I place here for the living,
That to this goal no one of them may hurry.
May they live on through full a thousand harvests,
And through this rock keep death away far from them.

—10. 18. 3. 4.

Now women with ointments enter the circle and approach the dead lying on the bier, to deck the widow, in token of her re-entrance into intercourse with the living. The priest summons her to separate herself from the corpse and himself takes the bow out of the hand of the dead man as the symbol of his ability, which they hope will remain in the community. The interment proceeds in fitting words and closes with the wish that the departed may find a place in the other world.

> The women here, still happy wives, not widowed,
> Shall come and bring rich oil and precious ointment;
> And tearless, blooming, rich adorned, may they first
> Approach the resting-place of the departed.
>
> Raise to the living world thy mind, O woman;
> His breath is fled and gone by whom thou sittest;
> Who took thee by the hand once and espoused thee,
> With him thy plighted troth is now accomplished.
>
> From out his lifeless hand his bow I've taken,
> A pledge to us of power, strength and honour,
> Thou yonder, and we here below as brave men,
> Shall overcome the force of every onslaught.
>
> Return once more unto the earth, thy mother,
> Her arms she opens kindly to receive thee,
> To good men kind and tender as a maiden,
> May she henceforth preserve thee from destruction.
>
> Firm may his spacious earthly home continue,
> Beneath supported by a thousand pillars,
> Let it henceforward be his house and riches,
> A sure protecting refuge for him ever.

I settle firmly now the earth about thee;
I cast the clods on thee,—let this not harm me.
The Fathers shall uphold these columns for thee,
But yonder Yama shall prepare a dwelling.
—10. 18. 7—13.

If we may not altogether look for **Historical Poems** among the ancestors of the Indian race, yet a number of songs of victory and triumph, most of them indeed only fragmentary, have been preserved to us. Although the really historical gain is not very rich and the statements are exceedingly deficient, these fragments still give us a glance into the active, war-disturbed life of the Vedic period. The individual clans, Aryan and non-Aryan, or even Aryans among themselves, oppress and drive each other from the homes just conquered; individual pretenders to a throne seek with armed hand to make their claims good or even dare to offer violence to a whole assembly with their band. Princes and clans form alliances to offer resistance to a too powerful ruler or, in later times, to throw off the yoke of the priest-class, ever becoming more oppressive.

The victorious princes love to hear their achievements praised in the loud song, and the singers soon know how to make their services indispensable; Indra, the ruler of battles, takes no pleasure in the Soma offered without prayer; he scorns the sacrificial food prepared without a song, and no mean song of praise finds favour with the divine dispensers of riches. Therefore the king who cannot himself prepare a proper song of praise is forced to seek the skill of others, and so we find, among the more important princes, singers and families of singers who first through their prayers make great deeds possible for the rulers and afterwards celebrate them. In the foreground of these families of singers stand those of Visvāmitra and Vasishṭha. The former had caused the rushing stream to stand still for the renowned Tṛtsu King Sudās, made the crossing possible for his patron and sent his steed forward to victory and spoils; but in course of time, pushed forward by the rising influence of his rival Vasishṭha, Visvāmitra went over to the gens of the Bharatas. With them he sets forth and comes to the junction of the rivers vipaś and śáturdrī, which stream lustily forth from the bosom of the mountains, racing, like two mares let loose. At the call and loud entreaty of the singer the waves yield, they make the passage easy and do not even moisten the axles with their billows. The host proceeds confidently to battle; then the singer, sprung from Kuśika, proudly proclaims: "My prayer, the prayer of Visvāmitra, protects the race of the Bharatas". But Indra prefers Vasishṭha; like ox-goads the haughty Bharatas are broken and the territory of the Tṛtsus is extended. And many other exploits Sudās accomplished with Vasishṭha's help; the wide-pouring river becomes a passable ford for Sudās, while the (pursuing?) insolent Śimyu becomes the sport of the waves.

The evil minded fools in other pathways
Turned from its course the rushing great Paruṣṇi.[1]
The lord of earth with mighty power seized them,
And prone upon the earth lay herd and shepherd.

At once the stream, their aim, was their destruction,
The swiftest even found rest beneath the waters.
There Indra into Sudās, hand gave over
His flying foes, the boasters to the strong man.

—7. 18. 8. 9.

[1] Name of a river.

The defiant Bheda is overcome, the Ajas and Sigrus and Yakshus bring the heads of the horses as tribute; Sudās conquers the challenging Pūrus in even fight, then takes the possessions of the Anus and from them and the people of the Druhyus sinks in sleep sixty hundred, six times a thousand spoilers, and sixty-six heroes in requital; ten kings had allied themselves and surrounded Sudās on all sides, but the adoring hymn of the guests (*i.e.*, the royal singers) was effectual; for the sake of the prayers of the Visishṭhids Indra rescued the prince. And many other fights are mentioned; Divodāsa quarrels with Śambara, and the Vetasu Daśadyu with the Taugras; the Bharatas war with the Pūrus, and on the Hariyūpiya the rearguard of the Vṛcîvants was scattered in fear when the van had been overcome; thirty hundred mailed Vṛcîvants, united at the Yavyāvatī full of ambition, fell by the arrow and sank into destruction, etc.

As sources of history may be mentioned also the so-called Dânastutis, *i.e.*, 'praise of gifts'. These are portions, not of the very highest poetical order, interpolated among or added to the real hymns, in which singers of an earlier period praise the generosity of the princes who bestowed presents on them. From these we not only see that these gifts were often considerable, but also discover the names of tribes and kings, together with indications of their homes; and some light is thrown on the families of singers and their genealogies. An example may be quoted here:

> In this the Ruśamas did well, O Agni,
> In that they gave me forty hundred cattle;
> The freely offered gift of Rinamcaya,
> Of heroes most heroic, we have taken.

The Ruśamas let me depart, O Agni,
Rewarded richly with a thousand cattle,
The sharp and gladdening juice made Indra merry,
When darkness lightened at the dawn of morning.

When darkness lightened at the dawn of morning,
From Rinamsaya, king of the Ruśamas,
Like speedy coursers, harnessed for the races,
Babhru received four times a thousand cattle.

Yea, forty hundred from the herds of cattle,
Did we, O Agni, get from the Ruśamas,
And, ready heated for our use in cooking,
A brazen pot did we receive, the singers.

—5. 30. 12-15.

Among the few **Humorous** pieces we find the jest of a poet, who banteringly likens the awakening of the frogs at the beginning of the rainy season, their merry croaking, and their jollity to the songs of priests intoxicated with soma, and to the noise of a school of priests.

The frogs were silent all the year,
Like Brāhmans fettered by a vow,
But now Parjanya calls them forth,
And loud their voices they uplift.

Soon as the rain from heaven has fallen on them,
Like shrivelled skins within the dry pool lying,
From all at once comes up a noisy croaking,
As when the cow calls to her calf with lowings.

When the first shower of the rainy season
Has fallen on them, parched with thirst and longing,
Then each with merry croak and loudly calling
Salutes the other, as a son his father.

One seizes and congratulates the other,
Delighted at the falling of the water,
In glee each wet and dripping frog jumps upward,
The green one and the speckled join their voices.

What one calls out, another quickly answers,
Like boys at school their teacher's words repeating.
Ye seem but many members of one body,
When in the pool ye lift your varied voices.

Some low like cattle, some like goats are bleating,
And one is yellow, and another speckled.
Alike in name, but various in appearance,
In many tones they modulate their voices.

Like priests attending at the Soma-offering,
Who sit around the full bowl, loudly singing,
Ye frogs around the pond hail the recurring
Of autumn when the rain-fall first commences.

They shout aloud like Brāhmans drunk with soma,
When they perform their annual devotions.
Like the Adhvaryu, sweating o'er the kettle,[41]
They issue forth,—not one remains in hiding.

The sacred order of the year observing,
These creatures never disregard the seasons;
When autumn comes and brings the time of showers,
They find release from heat and summer's scorching.

The frogs bleat like goats, and low like cattle,
The green one and the speckled, give us riches,
Whole herds of cows may they bestow upon us,[42]
And grant us length of days through sacrificing.

—7. 103.

In other places we meet with reflections upon the fact, that different as are the minds of men and various as their callings, yet all run after gain; for example, continues the author, he himself is a poet, papa a physician, and mama a miller; so in the most varied ways men chase after money. Another song makes us acquainted with a poet, who as poet, physician and apothecary in one person jurneys about the country, carrying with him in a wooden box all sorts of healing herbs, and plying his vocation not without humour; especially with a frankness that merits recognition he makes no secret of the fact that it is not altogether philanthrophy which urges him to practice; but that gain is his leading motive.

Two short hymns of the tenth book display fine perception and an intelligent interpretation of nature; one, to Rātri the Goddess of Night, describes how she, looking out from a thousand eyes, comes forth adorned with all the glory of the stars, fills heights and depths, and puts all, even the greedy bird of prey, to rest. The other sings of Araṇyāni, the mocking genius of the forest, and the solitude of the woods.

As an example of the secular poetry of that ancient time a few strophes of the well-known 'Dice-song' follows, the contents of which are indeed more tragic than humorous. A passionate player describes his propensity for the brown nuts;[43] he cannot free himself from them, though he sees well how much misery they produce for him and his.

> The nuts that once swayed on the lofty branches
> Intoxicate me, rolling on the dice-board.
> The fruit of the Vibhidaka can charm me,
> As 'twere the Soma of the Mūjantavas.[44]

My wife has never angered me nor striven,
Was ever kind to me and my companions;
Though she was faithful to me, I have spurned her,
For love of dice, the only thing I value.

My wife rejects me and her mother hates me;
The gamester finds no pity for his troubles.
No better use can I see for a gambler,
Than for a costly horse worn out and aged.

Upon his wife are laid the hands of others,
While his possessions by the dice are wasted.
His father, mother, brothers,—all deny him:
"We know him not, away with him in fetters".

The gambler's wife deserted mourns; his mother
Laments her son, she knows not where he wanders.
And he, in debt and trouble, seeking money,
Remains at night beneath the roof of strangers.

It grieves the gambler when he sees another
With wife and happy home untouched by trouble.
He yokes the brown steeds in the early morning
And when the fire goes out he sinks degraded.

And when I say that I will play no longer,
My friends abandon me and all desert me;
Yet when again I hear the brown dice rattling,
I hasten, like a wanton to her lover.

The gambler hurries to the gaming table,
"To-day I'll win," he thinks in his excitement.
The dice inflame his greed, his hopes mount higher;
He leaves his winnings all with his opponent.

—10. 34. 1—6. 10. 11.

Of **Didactic-Gnomic** poetry we find not a few products in the Rigveda. Experience repeatedly introduced is brought together in verse and lives as a 'winged word' in the mouths of all. It seems only a variation of the proverbs of our day when we read:

> The plough brings plenty when the soil it furrows;
> Who moves his feet accomplishes his journey;
> Speech benefits a Brâhman more than silence;
> A friend who gives is better than a niggard.
>
> —10. 11. 7.

The truth of the proposition: *Si duo faciunt idem, non est idem*, is confirmed in various directions, and it is commended as the "belssing of instruction," that "the straight path to the goal is found".

To Indra himself is ascribed the saying, "Woman's mind is hard to direct aright and her judgment too is small," while another has better words for women, and finds that may a man is better than his reputation.[45] "How many a maiden," reasons a singer, "is wooded only for her rich possessions", while another testifies "that even an ugly man is found beautiful, it only he is rich."[46] "Prudent and stupid, every one tries to export", seeks the greatest possible gain, without being fastidious in his methods,—this seems even at that time to have been the result of experience, as well as that "many a one brings gifts of sacrifice only thorugh fear of blame". But in other passages the duty and the blessing of good deeds are loudly proclaimed:

> Let him who can give succour to the needy,
> And well his future path of life consider.
> For fortune like the wheels of chariots rolling,
> Now, shifting, comes to one, now to another.
>
> —10 .117. 5.

By sharing with others one's own store is never decreased, and through beneficence a man gains to himself good friends for the changeful future. The so-called Song of Wisdom among other matters, reflects how many see without perceiving, how many hear without understanding, while for others all difficulties disappear of their own accord. The saying of Vāmadeva, "Not without pains are the gods made friends" could serve as admonition and encouragement, and on the other hand as recognition that "the rule of the gods is too high for man's wisdom; we men, all, are companions in death; speedily life runs away," and each one in death must abandon his wealth and become a solemn memento to to some one.

The **Formulas of Incantation** and **Exorism** may also be regarded as a kind of didactic poetry, although their proper department is really the Atharvaveda; but a number of such formulas are to be found in the Rig, *e.g.*, for healing the most various diseases. Such a '*mantra*' is repeated, and the healing of the sick person accomplished by the laying on of hands or some other ceremony; one who is near to death is recalled to life, an evil intention, a hostile demon, may be made harmless, a bad omen averted, a fortunate rival in love driven off, a herd gathered together again, etc.

Poetical Riddles

As a second branch of didacitic composition we must mention the **Poetical Riddles.** The simplest form is shown in a short hymn of the eighth book; from the very short description the gods meant can be guested, thus:

> One in his mighty hand holds fast the thunderbolt,
> With it his enemies he smites.

And one bears in his mighty hand a weapon shorp,
Yet kind withal, he seeks to heal.
Through empty space another made three mighty strides
Where the gods dwell in blessedness.

And two, with but one bride, on winged, steeds go forth,
They journey onward far away.

—8. 29. 4.5. 7.8.

Much more intricate and difficult, however, were the riddles and engines (*brahmodya*), which in latef Vedic time came into use at the great sacrifices of the kings, and at contests of various kinds. The priests propounded all sorts of questions from the whole circle of priestly knowledge, not only to the princes offering the sacrifice, but also to their companions in office, with whom they strove for pre-eminence. In these questions "the matters in discussion are usually not called by their ordinary, commonly understood names, but are indicated by symbolical expressions, or even only by mystical references, in which numbers play an important part. They are taken now from nature, now from the spiritual life. Heaven and earth, sun and moon, the atmosphere, the clouds, rain and its production by evaporation of the mists by means of the sun's rays, the sun's course, the year, the seasons, months, days and nights, are here favourite subjects of symbolic clothing; their interpretation is regarded as the highest wisdom.

With this enigmatical poetry the last group of hymns which have still to be mentioned, the **Philosophical Poetry,** stands in the closest connection. With few exceptions the compositions of this class are occupied with questions concerning the beginning and origin of all things, such queries occuring also here and there in the enigmatical hymns. A system of cosmogony is naturally not yet found here; they are throughout only first questions and attempts, the most primitive beginnings of natural philosophy and theories of creation. The poets like infants in their ignorance search with their intellect for the hidden traces of the invisible, unseen gods, for their origin and deeds. They are no longer satisfied with hearing that this or that god has created heaven and earth and fire and sun and dawn: in all seriousness "in order to know it, not for pastime alone," one asks; how many fires and how many suns, how many dawns and waters there are; whether day was created before night, or night before day, while another desires to know what tree it was, what kind of wood,[1] of which heaven and earth once were built, eternally firm, while days, many mornings, vanish; upon what the creator stood, when he upheld the worlds; what then was his standing-ground, what was the order of events, having made the earth out of what he enclosed the heavens with might. The question repeatedly appears, how and when from not-being the way was found to being, while others exert themselves to establish the beginning of all existent things, the original matter. The solution of these problems is naturally, where not evidently from the first shown to lie outside of human wisdom, very varied in result, and even the lines of development, if we may use the term, differ greatly. Sometimes fire, sometimes the all-nourishing water is named as the original matter, as among the Greek philosophers; in other passages an original germ is spoken of, which, on the other side of heaven and this earth and the living gods, the waters received into themselves, in which the gods all met.

[1]*i.e.*, the material, the original matter.

Far out beyond this earth, beyond the heavens,
Far, too, beyond the living gods and spirits,
What earliest germ was hidden in the waters,
In which the gods were all beheld together?

The waters held that earliest germ within them
In which the living gods were all united.
That One lay in the bosom of the unborn,
And all created beings rested in it.

Him ye can never know who formed these creatures,
Between yourselves and him lies yet another.
With stammering tongue and all in mist enveloped,
The singers go about in life rejoicing.

—10. 82. 5—7.

Another prominent hymn praises Hiraṇyagarbha, the 'gold-germ', as the kindly origin of all being, who existed even before the first breath of the gods, who alone is god among all the gods.

In the beginning rose Hiraṇyagarbha.
Born as the only lord of all existence.
This earth he settled firm and heaven established:
What god shall we adore with our oblations?

Who gives us breath, who gives us strength, whose bidding
All creatures must obey, the bright gods even;
Whose shade is death, whose shadow life immortal:
What god shall we adore with our oblations?

Who by his might alone became the monarch
Of all that breathes, of all that wakes or slumbers,
Of all, both man and beast, the lord eternal:
What god shall we adore with our oblations?

Whose might and majesty these snowy mountains,
The ocean and the distant stream exhibit;
Whose arms extended are these spreading regions:
What god shall we adore with our oblations?

Who made the heavens bright, the earth enduring,
Who fixed the firmament, the heaven of heavens;
Who measured out the air's extended spaces:
What god shall we adore with our oblations?

To whom with trembling mind the two great armies
Look up, by his eternal will supported;
On whom the sun sheds brightness in its rising:
What god shall we adore with our oblations?

—10. 121. 1—6.

The monotheistic conception lying at the foundation of this hymn appears more prominently, with the exception of some single verses in two hymns directed to Viśvakarman, *i.e.*, the 'All-creator' of unrivalled power of mind and body, to him.

Who is our father, our creator, maker,
Who every place doth know and every creature,
By whom alone to gods their names were given,
To him all other creatures go, to ask him.

—10. 82. 3.

By far the most important composition of this class in the whole Veda is the 'Song of Creation', recognized even by the Colebrooke.[47] In the beginning, when the contrasts of being and not-being, of death and immortality, of day and night, did not yet exist, only one thing hovered over the empty waste, and this one come into life through the force of heat; there the first germ of mind showed itself; then the wise ones, the cosmogonic gods, were able to call forth being out of not-being, and to separate and divide the heretofore unordered masses. But in spite of this solution the whole creation and many single things in it remain a riddle to the poet.

> Then there was neither being nor not-being.
> The atmosphere was not, nor sky above it.
> What covered all? and where? by what protected?
> Was there the fathomless abyss of waters?
>
> Then neither death nor deathlessness existed;
> Of day and night there was yet no distinction.
> Alone that One breathed calmly, self-supported,
> Other than It was none, nor aught above It.
>
> Darkness there was at first in darkness hidden;
> This universe was undistinguished water.
> That which in void and emptiness lay hidden
> Alone by power of fervour was developed.
>
> Then for the first time there arose desire,
> Which was the primal germ of mind, within it,
> And sages, searching in their heart, discovered
> In Nothing the connecting bond of Being.
>
> And straight across their cord was then extended:
> What then was there above? or what beneath it?
> Life giving principles and powers existed;
> Below the origin,—the striving upward.
>
> Who is it knows? Who here can tell us surely
> From what and how this universe has risen?
> And whether not till after it the gods lived?
> Who then can know from what it has arisen?

The source from which this universe has risen
And whether it was made, or uncreated,
He only knows, who from the highest heaven
Rules, the all-seeing lord,—or does not He know?
—10. 129.

We stand at the end of our survey. From it we ought to recognize that we have in the Rigveda a literature which well deserves 'at least in extracts to be known to every student and lover of antiquity', to every one who would have the poet's words, *Homo sum; humanum nihil a me alienum puto,* applied to himself. The chief importance of the Veda is not indeed for the history of literature, but it lies elsewhere; it lies, as the following commentary seeks to show, in the very extraordinary fullness of disclosures which this unique book gives to the student of philosophy and the history of civilization. In this, no other literature is to be compared with it, and though the aestheic value of this relic of long-vanished times has sometimes been exaggerated, yet its historical importance, its value for the history of mankind, cannot easily be overrated.

NOTES

[1] *Essai sur les mœurs et l'esprit des nations.*

[2] *Ideen Zur Geschichte der Menschheit.*

[3] *Zur Litteratur und Geschichte des Weda, Drei Abhandlungen.*

[4] *Academische Vorlesungen über indische Literaturgeschichte.*

[5] This is the favourite sacrifice of the Vedic period, at which the sap of the soma plant, mixed with milk or barley, was offered.

[6] The two principal groups of these prayer-books, the *Black* and the *White Yajurveda,* are essentially distinguished by the fact that in the Black the sacrificial verses are followed immediately by their dogmatic interpretation, description of the accompanying ritual, etc., and the Brâhmaṇa belonging to it is to be considered as an addition differing only in time; while in the White the verses for the sacrifices are contained in the Sanhitâ, the interpretation and ritual in the Brâhmaṇa and thus are separated throughout.

[7] Concerning these books Muller, ASL. 389, says: "The Brâhmaṇas represent no doubt a most interesting phase in the history of the Indian mind, but judged by themselves as literary productions, they are most disappointing. No one would have supposed that at so early a period, and in so primitive a state of society, there could have risen up a literature which, for pedantry and downright absurdity can hardly be matched anywhere. There is no lack of striking thoughts, of bold expressions, of sound reasoning, and curious traditions in these collections. But they are only like the fragments of a torso, like precious gems set in brass and lead. The general character of these works is marked by shallow and insipid grandiloquence, by priestly conceit and antiquarian pedantry. It is most important to the historian that he should know how soon the fresh and healthy growth of a nation can be blighted by priestcraft and superstition.

These works deserve to be studied as the physician studies the twaddle of idiots and the raving of madmen."

[8] The later development of the ruling priesthood recognizes four stages (*âshrama*) in the life of the Brâhmaṇa; first he is a *brahmachârin* (disciple of a Brâhmaṇa), then a *gṛihastha* (married, father of a family), then a *vânaprastha,* and finally a *bhikṣu* or *sannyâsin* (a begger living on alms, who has denied the world).

[9] I believe I shall not be contradicted by Helmholtz, or Ellis, or other representatives of phonetic science, if I say that, to the present day, the phoneticians of India of the fifth century B.C. are unsurpassed in their analysis of the elements of language—Max Muller O. G. R. 150.

[10] The Gṛihyasûtras, of which only a few have been published, will have the greatest importance for the comparative study of customs: with their aid it will be possible to show that many customs, whether in the life of the classic nations, in the ritual of the Catholic church, or in the common life of the present day, come from primeval times.

[11] The degree to which the understanding of these texts had been lost may be illustrated by a literary strife between Yâska and another Vedic scholar, Kautsa. The latter insisted that explanation of the words was useless, since the hymns had no meaning at all; to which Yâska responded, that it was not the fault of the rafter that the blind man did not see it; that was the fault of the blind man.

[12] *Altindisches Leben,* Berlin, 1879.

[13] Whereas formerly Asia, especially the highland of Central Asia, the region of the sources of the Oxus and Yaxartes was in general held to be the original as well as the last home of the Indogermanic people while they were still living together, other investigators in later times thought they had grounds for seeking it in Europe.

[14] The older Indian chronology presents great difficulties. The determination of the Vedic period must be deduced from the histories of the various literatures which lie between the hymns and the fixed dates of Buddhism, from the differnce in language and in the

religious and social views between the former and latter, and can therefore approximate the true period only by centuries.

[15] *Treatment of the Aged*: "Among the Germans, when the master of the house was over sixty years old, if the signs of the weakness of age were of such a character that he 'no longer had the power to walk or stand, and to ride unassisted and unsupported, with collected mind free will and good sense,' he was obliged to give over his authority to his son, and to perform menial service; then old men might be made by hard sons and cruel grandsons to expiate painfully the love and gentleness they had neglected in their more powerful days; those who had grown useless and burdensome were even either killed outright, or exposed and abandoned to death by starvation."

"Exactly similar things are told by the attendants of Alexander the Great of Iranian tribes, and even among the Romans there was a period when old men over sixty were thrown down from the bridge into the Tiber."

Burning of Widows: The death of the wife with her departed husband as an old custom (*dharma purâna*). —But that this custom was not general, other passages beside RV. 10, 18, 7, show, which prove the re-marriage of the widow (AV. 9, 5, 27,—with her brother-in-law: RV. 10, 40, 2: levirate marriage), and that the usage only received decided sanction in late times, is evident from the fact that "the Indian law literature, from the oldest times up to the late period, treats fully of the widow's right of inheritance, and that the isolated references to the burning of widows in some of the law-books endorse it only as a matter of choice."

[16] *Writing, its use*: It may now be considered as proved that the Vedic texts were for a long time transmitted orally and were only at a comparatively late date fixed in a written form (cf. Note 76) that the Indian alphabets are of Semitic origin, and that the application of writing to literary uses arose chiefly with Buddhism.

[17] *Relative age of the separate books*: H. Brunnhofer publishes the first very valuable attempt to collect the indications of the Vedic language (especially the uses of

the various infinitival formations) in a methodical manner for the determination of the relative age of the various collections of hymns (family books, etc.). He gets the following chronological order of the families of singers:

1. Gautamas: Maṇḍ. 4 (principal poet Vâmadeva).
2. Bhârâdvajas: Maṇḍ. 6.
3. Vâsiṣṭhas: Maṇḍ. 7.
4. Ātreyas: Maṇḍ. 5.
5. Vaicvâmitras: Maṇḍ. 3.
6. Bhârgavas: Maṇḍ. 2 (principal poet Gṛtsamada).
7. Āngirasas: portions of Maṇḍ. 1. 8. 9. 10.
8. Káṇvas: portions of Maṇḍ. 1. 8. 9.

The poet's names handed down for books 2—8 may, in general, be correct; yet even here, but especially in the later books, it is evident that many of them have simply been got out of the hymns by ingenuity, of which we have examples enough in other literatures.

[18] It is a peculiarity of the Sanskrit that adjoining words in a sentence are united with each other according to certain laws, by which their initial and final portions are subjected to various changes through assimilation, elision, etc., which naturally cause difficulties in understanding; these it was sought to obviate by fixing the text, not only in the ordinary *connected form* (*Sanhitâ-pâṭha*), but also in an *unconnected* (*Pada-pâṭha, word-text*), which gave the separate words as each originally appeared, independently; thus we have presented to us in the Pada-pâṭha one of the first exegetical works. But soon the two pâṭhas named appeared no longer sufficient; new ones were made, in part very complicated, in order to make every alteration of the sacred text absolutely impossible. Three of these forms of the text may be mentioned:

The *Kramapâṭha* ('step-text') puts each word of the Pada-pâṭha twice: first, in connection with the preceding words; next, with the succeeding, so that the order a b c d gives the Krama members ab, bc, cd; the Krama is treated by the Upalekha.

The *Jáṭapâṭha* ('the woven text) exhibits each Krama member three times, the second time in reversed order: ab, ba, ab, bc. cb. bc, cd. dc. cd; the Jaṭâ is treated in the Jaṭâpaṭala, herausgegeben, übersetzt und mit Aumerkungen versehen von G. Thibaut, Leipzig 1870.

The *Ghanapâtha* shows the order: ab. ba. abc. cba. abc, bc. cb. bcb. dcb. bc, bc. cb. bcd. dcb. bcd, etc.; for the Ghana.

Senseless as such endless repetitions are in themselves, they still have this value for us, that they fix absolutely the wording of the text, and in that, indeed, their purpose is accomplished.

[19] Sanskrit is the *artificial, adorned speech* of the three higher castes and the learned literary language in distinction to the *popular dialect, Prâkrit.* It is used in the Indian drama only by gods and male members of the first two castes, priests and warriors, while all females (including goddesses), children, and people of lower class speak Prâkrit.

[20] Westphal has shown that the Indo-Germanic period possessed a kind of poetry the metrical principle of which was the counting of syllables. This syllabic system is found in pure and unmodified form only in the Iranian people, in the metrical portions of the Avesta. The prosody of the Vedas shows the first advance, the transition from metre depending only on the number of syllables to one based on quantity, in which the beginning still shows the stage of mere syllable-counting, while the ending has attained prosodical fixedness. The latter in the case of the Greeks meets us from the commencement of the literature fully developed and as the first principle of metrical composition (as also the metres of later Indian poetry are altogether quantitative). 'But in one point, even with Greeks, is shown a remnant of that stage, preceding the perfected prosodical metre, upon which they anciently stood together with the Indians. Among the Indians the first half of the Dimeter is prosoodically undefined, among the Greeks the first half of the Dipody, where the trochee may interchange with spondee. The "free base" of the Aeolians may also be referred to this stage' (Westphal). In correction of Westphal, Allen has shown that "the common ancestors of Germans, Indians and Iranians sang their ballads in a

verse which consisted of two sharply separated members, of which each had four ictus and four light syllables; and each member began with a light syllable and closed with an ictus". To this verse Allen further refers the Homeric Hexameter and the Italic Saturnian verse.

[21]In so far as we are Aryans in speech, that is, in thought, so far the Rigveda is our own oldest book."—Max Muller.

[22]"The Indians developed their religion to a kind of old-world classicity, which makes it for all time the key of the religious beliefs of all mankind".

[23]Such a presentation of the Vedic mythology, after *de Gubernatis' Letture sopra la Mitologia vedica,* Firenze 1874, is greatly to be desired, but presupposes a number of special investigations. Abel Bergaigne's work, *La Religion Védique d'apres les Hymnes du Rigveda,* Paris 1878-1883, contains a number of correct remarks and observations on particulars, but, according to our view, is too much dominated by preconceived opinions, and does not even claim to offer such a presentation. The best, most copious and reliable sources are the excellent Original Sanskrit Texts on the Origin and History of the people of India, their Religion and Institutions. Collected, translated and illustrated by John Muir, especially vols. 4 and 5.

[24]Ubersetzt von Karl Geldner and Adolf Kaegi. Mit Beiträgen von R. Roth, Tabingen, 1875.

[25] *Agohya* is the "unconcealable" sun-god, with whom the Rbhus rest after their year's course; *i.e.,* the year is at an end; the three seasons and the sun, which has reached its lowest point, apparently rest twelve days,—the twelve intercalary days of the winter solstice.

[26]Demigods, mediators between gods and men.

[27]Max Muller, who traced a very large number of myths to the Dawn, says "The dawn which to us is merely a beautiful sight, was, to the early gazer and thinker, the problem of all problems. It was the unknown land from whence rose every day those bright emblems of a divine power which left in the mind of man the first impression and intimation of another world, of power above, of order and

wisdom. What we simply call the sunrise, brought before their eyes every day the riddle of all riddles, the riddle of existence. The days of their life sprang from that dark abyss, which every morning seemed instinct with light and life. Their youth, their manhood, their old age, all were to the Vedic bards the gift of that heavenly mother who appeared bright, young, unchanged, immortal, every morning, while everything else seemed to grow old, to change, and droop, and at last to set, never to return. It was there, in that bright chamber, that, as their poets said, mornings and days were spun, or, under a different image, where mornings and days were nourished, where life or time was drawn out. It was there that the mortal wished to go, to meet Mitra and Varuṇa. The whole theogony and philosophy of the ancient world centred in the Dawn, the mother of the bright gods, of the sun in his various aspects, of the morn, the day, the spring; herself the brilliant image and visage of immortality."

[28]Hillebrant rightly observes, "To infer from the name that they were all personifications of various attributes of the sun, seems suspicious to me, in so far as we look upon it as a production of the Vedic poets themselves; for some, we may rather ask whether they were not originally sun-gods of different tribes, who gave them names as they appealed to their fancy; whether, then, in the consolidation of single tribes, the cults were not also brought over," etc.

[29]Pûsan:—"The strong lord of refreshing, the strong friend of nourishing"; "Give richly, and with open hand"; "We call him, that he may be a true defender and guardian for the increase of wealth";

Muir says—"We pray to thee for happiness
From trouble free, in treasures rich;
For full prosperity to-day,
And for to-morrow highest good."

[30]Do the passages 6, 56, 1; 1, 138, 4; 1, 42, 10.
Who mockingly of. Pusan says:
'Behold the gruel-eater there'
His jeers the god will not endure.
For I do not disdain thee, Pusan, glowing god;
Thy friendship I do not reject.

The god from us no chiding hears;
We bring him praise in pleasing songs,
The helper we implore for wealth,

indicate mockery on the part of certain tribes towards those with other cults?

[31]Bring us, to Pusan, to a man
Who, wise, at once shall point the way,
And say to us, "Lo, here it is."
With Pusan joined let us go forth,
Who points the houses out to us,
And says to us: "Lo, here they are."

[32]To Savitar is also addressed the celebrated Gayatri or Savitri, the daily prayer of the Brahmans: "Of Savitar, the heavenly, that longed for glory may we win and may himself inspire our prayers!" "No good and sufficient explanation of the peculiar sanctity attaching to this verse has ever been given; it is not made remarkable either by thought or diction, among many other Vedic verses of similar tenor. Its meaning is a matter of some question, depending on the meaning given to the verb in the second pada, *dhimahi,* whether we may receive, gain, win, or 'let us meditate.' If the latter be correct, the correspondence of root and meaning between this verb and the following noun, *dhiyah,* in the third pada, cannot be accidental, and should be regarded in translating: we must read, "and may he inspire (or quicken) our meditations (adoring or prayerful thoughts)." "Sayaṇa gives no less than four different explanations of the *gâyatri,* and leaves his readers free choice as to which they will accept."

[33]Aditi:—"And thee I summon to my side,
O mighty goddess, Aditi,
Thee, Merciful, to my defence.

In deep or shallow places save,
Thou mother of the gods, from foes,
Do thou our children keep from harm.

Far-searching thou, grant sure defence
To all our children, far and wide,
That, living, they may spread abroad."

Aditi, viewed as a divinity, as the personification of 'the visible Infinite, the endless expanse beyond the earth, beyond the clouds, beyond the sky' (Muller, Translation 1, 230) may be younger than Varuṇa, Bhaga, Mitra, and Aryaman; but the group of the Adityas, as the name itself proves, presupposes the proper name Aditi (Weber, JLZ. 1876, p. 652-IStr. 3, 453). "It was, no doubt the frequent mention of these her sons that gave to Aditi, almost from the beginning, a decidedly feminine character. She is the mother with powerful, with terrible, with royal sons. But there are passages where Aditi seems to be conceived as a male deity or, anyhow, as a sexless being." Muller, OGR. 236 f.

Aditi is praised in pantheistic fashion in 1, 89, 10; "Aditi is the heaven Aditi the atmosphere, Aditi, the mother; she (*sá*) is father, she son, all gods are Aditi, the whole world, Aditi is what is born, Aditi is what shall be born," recalling the familiar Orphic verses.

[34]"The laws of the moral are as eternal and unchangeable as those of the natural world. The same divine power has established the one and the other. This power is represented by a circle of divinites who may be most pertinently entitled the Gods of Heavenly Light. Human imagination was able to find no visible thing with which they could be compared, saving the light. They are and are named the Spiritual."—Roth

[35]"From the broad earth and from the heights of heaven
Ye send abroad your spies that never tire,
In every place, through field and house, their presence
Unceasingly keeps watch on each transgressor.

All your avenging spirits, O ye Mighty,
In whom can be perceived no form or token,
Unerringly the sin of men they punish;
And nothing is so hid as to escape you."

[36].We must admit that in no other natural religion, with the single exception of the Iranian, which is only another branch of the same family, were the nature and the guilt of sin fixed more firmly and weighed more gravely. A religion which makes its highest divinity gaze into the deepest secrets of the human heart,—how could a

recognition of the nature and guilt of sin escape it? Sin is a consequence of human weakness as well as of human wickedness, but as sin it is not less punishable in one case than in the other; and forgiveness is sought of Varuna even for sins which have been done in ignorance. And more than once we find in these old hymns penitent confessions of sin, united with prayer for forgiveness, expressed in the speech of simple faith. The guilt of sin is felt as a burdensome fetter, and freedom from its servitude is prayed for; here as elsewhere human power can accomplish nothing without divine assistance, for by himself man has not the power even to open or close his eyes." —Roth.

[37] "It is nowhere clearly and distinctly expressed as the teaching of this religion, that the wages of sin is death in the sense that men die only in consequence of their guilt, and that without it they would live eternally; but the thought is often very nearly touched. Immortality is the free gift of divine mercy to men."—Roth.

[38] The heaven is, therefore, the home of the soul, to which, after death, it returns purified ("free from all imperfections")

"Let the eye go to the sun, thy breath to the wind; go to the sky, to the earth, according to (thy) nature; go to the waters, if that is destined for thee; enter into the plants with thy members."—10, 16, 3.

[39] Whitney remarks:—"The simple-minded Aryan people, whose whole religion was a worship of the wonderful powers and phenomena of nature, had no sooner perceived that this liquid had power to elevate the spirits and produce a temporary frenzy, under the influence of which the individual was prompted to, and capable of deeds beyond his natural powers, than they found in it something divine; it was to their apprehension a god, endowing those into whom it entered with godlike powers; the plant which afforded it became to them the king of plants. . . . Soma is addressed in the highest strains of adulation and veneration; all powers belong to him; all blessings are besought of him, as his to bestow, etc."

[40] Prajapati, 'lord of descendants,' a genius presiding over birth, then in general protector of the living, and

afterward 'lord of creatures, creator,' as highest good over the mentioned gods of the Vedic period.

[41]The priest who offers the prayers and praises (ṛcas) at the sacrifice is the hotar, the speaking priest; the adhvaryu, the acting priest performs the sacrifice.

[42]This verse appears to have been added in order to give the hymn the appearance of a prayer.

[43]For dice the brown nuts of the Terminalia bellerica were used, the taste of which intoxicates, just as their use as dice enthrals the gambler's senses.

[44]A tribe living on the mountain Mūjavant in the western Himâlayas.

[45]"There can be no friendship with women, their hearts are those of hyenas"; on the other hand, the more favorable verdict, "And many a woman is often better than the man, the godless, impious; she, who knows well how to distinguish the weary, the thirsty, and lovers (i.e. helps and assists each in the right way), and has turned her mind to the gods."

[46]"To how many a maiden does the wooer, who desires to become her husband, show affection for the sake of her admirable treasures; but if a woman is pure and beautiful, she can of herself (even without treasure) find her mate in the people."—10, 27, 12.

[47]Whitney says:—"The general character and value of the hymn are very clear. It is of the highest historical interest as the earliest known beginning of such speculation in India, or probably anywhere among Indo-European races. The attitude of its author and the audacity of his attempt are exceedingly noteworthy. But nothing can be said in absolute commendation of the success of the attempt. On the contrary, it exhibits the characteristic weaknesses of all Hindu theosophy; a disposition to deal with words as if they were things, to put forth paradox and insoluble contradiction as profundity. . . . The unlimited praises which have been bestowed upon it, as philosophy and poetry, are well-nigh nauseating."—Verse 2: "Whether 'fervour' (tapas) means physical heat or devotional ardour, penance, according to the later prevalent meaning of the word, admits of a question; but it is doubtless to be under

stood in the Hindu cosmogonies, while penance, the practice of religious austerities, is a constant factor in their theories."—Verse 5: "But the next verse is still more unintelligible; no one has ever succeeded in putting any sense into it, and it seems so unconnected with the rest of the hymn that its absence is heartily to be wished. 'Crosswise (was) stretched out the ray (line) of them: was it, forsooth, below? was it, forsooth, above? impregnators were, greatness were; *svadhâ* below, offering beyond.' The word rendered 'offering' is literally 'forth reaching,' and, as sometimes also, as perhaps here, the signification 'straining, intentness.' . . . Who, the 'they' are, unless the sages of the preceding verse, it is hard to guess".

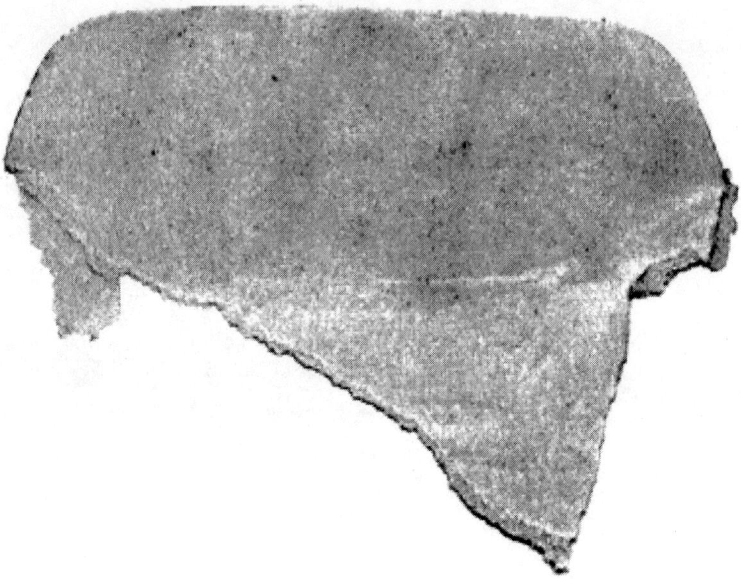